Letters to Lydia

Words of Advice from a Grandfather to His Grandchildren

CHUCK TANK

LITTLE CREEK PRESS
AND BOOK DESIGN

Mineral Point, Wisconsin USA

Copyright © 2018 Chuck Tank

Little Creek Press® Book Design
A Division of Kristin Mitchell Design, Inc.
5341 Sunny Ridge Road
Mineral Point, Wisconsin 53565

Book Design and Project Coordination:
Little Creek Press and Book Design

First Edition
January 2018

All rights reserved

No part of this book may be used or reproduced
in any manner whatsoever without written
permission from the author.

Printed in Wisconsin, United States of America

For more information or to order books,
email: chucktank1975@gmail.com
or visit: www.littlecreekpress.com

Library of Congress Control Number: 2017962713

ISBN-10: 1-942586-30-2
ISBN-13: 978-1-942586-30-2

To Becky,
without whom this book would
have never been written.

Table of Contents

INTRODUCTION 7

PART 1: YOUR HISTORY 10
    Chapter 1: Who Are You? 11
    Chapter 2: Who Am I? 16
    Chapter 3: The First Time I Held You 21
    Chapter 4: What Was Your Mom Like? 24
    Chapter 5: What Was Your Dad Like? 28
    Chapter 6: Tank Humor 32

PART 2: THINGS TO CONSIDER AS
YOU GO THROUGH LIFE 36
    Chapter 7: The Important Things 37
    Chapter 8: Finding Your Passion in Life 40
    Chapter 9: Setting Goals and Chasing Your Dreams 43
    Chapter 10: Being a Good Person 46
    Chapter 11: Honesty 49
    Chapter 12: Ethics 52
    Chapter 13: Change 56
    Chapter 14: Being Happy 59
    Chapter 15: Sports 62
    Chapter 16: Fears 67
    Chapter 17: Education 71
    Chapter 18: Reading 75
    Chapter 19: Religion 81
    Chapter 20: Pleasing Your Parents 86
    Chapter 21: Toughness 89
    Chapter 22: Work Ethic 93
    Chapter 23: Entitlement 97
    Chapter 24: Choices 101

Chapter 25: Control the Things You Can Control......... 105
Chapter 26: Helping Others............................ 109
Chapter 27: Being Stubborn............................ 113
Chapter 28: Eating.................................... 116
Chapter 29: Time...................................... 120
Chapter 30: Drinking and Drugs........................ 124
Chapter 31: Priorities................................ 128
Chapter 32: Money..................................... 131
Chapter 33: Invisible Elephant in the Room............ 135
Chapter 34: Little Things............................. 138
Chapter 35: At the Ocean 141
Chapter 36: Midwestern Values......................... 145
Chapter 37: Schmoozers................................ 148
Chapter 38: Being the Rock............................ 152
Chapter 39: Regrets 155
Chapter 40: Death 158

PART 3: RELATIONSHIPS 162
Chapter 41: Death 163
Chapter 42: Family Traditions......................... 166
Chapter 43: Red Flags, Green Flags.................... 170
Chapter 44: Love and Looks............................ 174
Chapter 45: Dating.................................... 177
Chapter 46: Getting Your Heart Broken................. 181
Chapter 47: Mean People............................... 185
Chapter 48: Abuse 188
Chapter 49: Communication............................. 191
Chapter 50: Finding the Love of Your Life............. 194
Chapter 51: Marriage.................................. 198
Chapter 52: A Final Letter to Lydia 202
Acknowledgements...................................... 205
Alleman-Tank Family Tree.............................. 206
About the Author...................................... 208

Introduction

I had the thought to write some words of advice in the fall of 2016 just after I turned 60 years old. That's all this book is really, words of advice from a grandfather who has lived a long time to my grandchildren, especially granddaughter, Lydia, born earlier that year. I hope that this book provides them with some insight into who they are, where they come from, and how to handle some of the issues in life they are sure to face in the twenty-first century. Certainly my grandchildren may not agree with some of my thoughts and have every right not to follow these words as the gospel truth. I do hope my grandchildren will reflect on my words as they go through life and make positive decisions about issues which I have already faced. While this is intended to be a book written to all my grandchildren, for convenience sake and because the title is *Letters to Lydia,* I will address topics specifically to her.

While reading books does not always seem to be the way to learn in today's world, for many years I have been an avid reader, and I always thought that I could write a book as well, although the task always looked daunting. Ten years ago, in 2007, while I was still a high school boys varsity basketball coach in Dodgeville, Wisconsin, I wrote *Coaching Our Sons,* a book chronicling my own experiences coaching high school basketball as well as those of numerous other coaches who had their own sons on their teams. The experience of writing a book, finding a publisher willing to publish it, and then marketing the finished product taught me a lot. (One comment was that it was easier to get an audience with the Pope than it was to get someone to publish your book.) Writing that book was one of my bucket list accomplishments.

Since then, both of my daughters, Alli and Ann, have graduated from high school and college. Both are teachers and have married two fine young men. Lydia Jeanne Alleman, born on May 17, 2016, is Ann's daughter and my first grandchild. When I look into her smiling eyes, I see my own past as well as my own mortality. I also see her future. While I cannot predict the events that will shape her life, I do know that her life is in front of her, and in writing *Letters to Lydia*, I am trying to provide her with a "heads-up" on many of life's challenges.

Meanwhile, some friends and especially my wife, Becky, have asked me when I am going to write my second book and what it's going to be about. Couldn't it be a book about some part of history, a topic I have spent thirty-eight years teaching to my high school kids? Others have speculated that I could write about what it's like teaching in today's world in which social media and other avenues of technology command the attention of so many. Or perhaps I could write about parenting since all three of my children have grown into well-established adults.

For some time, I internally debated. I wasn't sure what to do. Writing a book had been much more difficult than I had anticipated, and I just wasn't ready to accept the next challenge. That is, until May 18, 2016, the first day I got to hold my granddaughter. When I held her and spoke to her for the first time, I knew that I wanted to tell her what life was all about. I wondered if I would be around to experience some of life's highs and lows with her. While I was not sure how long I would be there, I knew that to me she was special, and I wanted her to know a few things.

Much to my daughters' dismay, "Tank men die young" has been a saying my family has heard for years. My dad, Bill Tank, was only sixty-four when we lost him. His father, the grandfather I never got to know, was only sixty-three. Two of my brothers, Jim and Jon, passed away at ages sixty-nine and fifty-three. Only my older brother Mike and I survive our original family. While I do not have my own personal death wish, I do wonder if I will survive for another twenty years to be eighty when Lydia will be twenty. Obviously, I hope I do. If not, this is the primary reason I chose to write *Letters to Lydia*. I want her to know who I am and what I have learned. She is part of my blood.

You will notice that this book is made up of a series of interrelated topics. The first thing I did after conceiving the idea for this book was to begin jotting down different ideas of importance to me as well as to Lydia at different times throughout her life. The first question was if I was not around, what would you ask me? Of course, I can only speculate as to what those questions would be. With that in mind, I began putting together some of the chapters revolving around questions and advice I deemed most important.

I tried to divide my thoughts and words of advice into three separate categories. The first is Lydia's own personal history. I believe that people who have a solid understanding of who they are and where they come from have a distinct advantage over those who do not. I want Lydia to know who she is.

The second broad category of advice in *Letters to Lydia* is how to live your life. What are potential roadblocks she might run into and how can she handle them? While I understand that I may not be there for her every step of the way, I want her to know that I too have faced difficult situations and share how I dealt with them. I especially want her to understand that when things in her life don't go her way and may get worse for a time, just to fight through it, and it will get better.

Relationships started out as a smaller topic to be addressed but very quickly became the third major category for *Letters to Lydia*. Your relationships with people are so important in your life. The people with whom you choose to relate and associate with have a tremendous impact on the person you become. As I said earlier, I feel so fortunate that my daughters have chosen good husbands. I see teenage guys every day in my career. I could not be happier with the two young men my daughters have married. Unless Wes decides to become a father, they will be the fathers of my grandchildren.

CHAPTER 1:
Who Are You?

*"On matters of style, swim with the current;
on matters of principle, stand like a rock."*

– Thomas Jefferson

Dear Lydia:

I think the most valuable thing you can do is learn about yourself. If you're sixteen when you read this, you probably think, "I already get it, Grandfather. I know who I am." You may think you do, but how much about your past do you really know? The more you know about your past, the more you will know about yourself. What kind of people were your great-grandparents? Everyone has strengths, and everyone has weaknesses. Do you understand yours and how they came to be?

Your great-grandparents on your mom's side of the family were Bill Tank (1916–1981) and Lydia Tank, yes, your namesake, (1921–1980), and Phil Thompson and Mary Jane Thompson.

Bill and Lydia Tank were both part of what became known as the "Greatest Generation." Born to German immigrants in Sheboygan, Wisconsin, they grew to adulthood during two of the most difficult periods of American history, the Great Depression of the 1930s and World War II of the 1940s. Perhaps because of their experiences as members of families who were forced to endure hardship, they became strong, blue-collar people who were devoted to their family and their faith. Together, following the war, they raised four boys, each six years apart, in Sheboygan Falls, Wisconsin.

Your great-grandmother Lydia was a very special woman. Several things made her so. For a few years during the war in the 1940s, she worked as a "Rosie the Riveter" at the Kohler Company as Sheboygan County's men went off to fight the war. Following the war, Lydia met Bill Tank, who had come back after serving in London, England, where Bill had met an Englishwoman, with whom their son, Jim, was born in 1945. Bill and his English bride had come back to Wisconsin after the war, but their marriage did not last. In 1949, Bill courted and married Lydia in Sheboygan. The marriage would last for the rest of their lives, and it was a good one. They stuck by and supported each other through numerous health issues.

There is a strong artistic strain in the family, which descends from Grandma Lydia Tank's line of the family. Lydia and her brother, Ed Seidenzahl, loved to draw, and as a boy I recall my mother hosting drawing contests for the neighborhood children. Lydia's youngest son and my younger brother Jon was an extremely talented artist. Your Aunt Alli and Uncle Wes are known for their artistic flair.

The night you were born through an extremely complicated birth, Dr. Hostetler, the doctor who delivered you, held you while quietly rocking you and whispering to you. It had been touch and go for a time for both you and your mom. Thankfully you had survived, and she wanted you to be named after a strong person. Your grandmother Lydia Tank had just that strength of character. Over the last seventeen years or so of her life she had a disease called purpura, a blood disorder in which her vessels would often burst, creating bright red blotches on various parts of her body, including her face. While various parts of her body would swell and look distorted, she would also become violently ill and be bedridden or hospitalized (doctors made house calls then) for two or three days. She endured this once a month or so for seventeen years. I watched her go through this throughout my teen and college years. What strikes me most, however, was the fact that she never complained. She was most thankful to all the health care people and family members who helped out when she had one of her episodes. I have never seen anyone take so much without complaint. She was the toughest person I have ever known. Lydia Tank died on September 4, 1980, at age fifty-nine.

Bill Tank was born in 1916 and raised in Sheboygan, Wisconsin. Fortunately, he survived the great flu epidemic following World War I in which millions of people died. Bill was a strong, athletic guy who loved all sports. During World War II, your great-grandfather enlisted so he could serve in the military police. He spent time in London, England, during the Battle of Britain.

Lydia and Bill's marriage, which began in Sheboygan Falls in 1949, was a good one. While Bill worked long hours for many years as a foreman in the Pottery Division of the famous Kohler Company, Lydia also spent a considerable amount of time being a nanny for the famous Kohler family. She had a special knack with little kids. She could relate well with them, and they loved her. She also had a special place in her heart for children with special needs. I do not think it's coincidental that I went on to become a teacher for thirty-eight years (and still going), and your mom and Aunt Alli are also teachers who work well with young children. I believe that connection is there. Kids know very quickly if you like them or not.

My mom and dad's life revolved around their four kids, each born about six years apart: Jim, 1945–2015; Mike, born in 1950; myself, born in 1956; and Jon, 1962–2016. As Bill and Lydia got older, I remember them saying how great it was when all of us were together for a Wisconsin brat fry on a Sunday. (To this day, I love eating brats and have told nearly mythical but true stories of Bill eating a triple brat on a hard roll. Grandma Becky, a passionate cardiac rehab nurse, was dismayed.)

They lived in five homes throughout their marriage from 1949 until Lydia's death in 1980, all in the small town of Sheboygan Falls. We didn't have a lot. My parents were forced to sell the beautiful new home they built during the early 1960s to pay my mom's mounting medical bills. It took two trips to the Mayo Clinic in Rochester, Minnesota, to diagnose her pervading illness. They were under tremendous stress yet they faced it together. What I remember the most about those years is that we must have been poor, but I never knew it. We always had food on the table. My dad never owned a new car, but we always had one. During the last years of their lives, our family lived strictly on Social Security benefit money, for which I will be forever thankful.

One of the letters of advice I wanted to pass on and will address in another chapter regards the issue of entitlement. So many kids, and adults act like they are entitled to one thing or another, and somehow their parents buckle and give in to them. When I think of my parents, this angers me. For example, my birthday is October 3, when the baseball season is heading into the playoffs, the football season is heading into high gear, and basketball season is just around the corner. One year I can remember being unable to decide if I wanted to ask for a new baseball bat or a football for my birthday. To my surprise, I got both. I was thrilled! The point is, Lydia, don't feel entitled.

Your Great-Grandma Lydia Tank loved to garden and especially enjoyed flowers. In August 1980, when your Grandma Becky and I were only married for eight months, and I was preparing to begin my second year in teaching, Lydia was working in her flower garden when she accidentally stumbled backward, fell slightly and bumped her head. Within days the family could tell that something was wrong. At first, some of us thought that the issue was another one of her medical episodes. Within a day or so, Lydia was beginning to have trouble speaking, and the thought was a possible stroke. She was to be transferred from Sheboygan Memorial Hospital to Columbia Hospital in Milwaukee. Before she left, I went into her hospital room to see her, not knowing if she could even communicate with me or hear me. I sat there for a short time alone with her when she briefly regained consciousness and looked directly at me. I told her I loved her. She looked scared, was unsure of what was happening, and was having a difficult time forming words. She looked directly at me and determinedly said her last words to me, "I love you."

Lydia Tank slipped into a two-week coma from which she never regained consciousness. She died two weeks later on September 4, 1980, at Columbia Hospital in Milwaukee. Your Great-Grandfather Bill Tank was crushed by the loss of his wife. She was the rock of their relationship. Without her, Bill, whose health was also unstable at best, went downhill quickly. He made it known that he did not want to live without her, and he gave up. I only remember seeing my dad cry twice during my life. The first time was the day after my mother died. He sat at the kitchen table with his face in his hands and wept. The second time was at the Christmas Eve service at St. Paul's Lutheran Church in Sheboygan Falls that same year. As we sang the candlelight version of "Silent Night," my mother's favorite Christmas hymn, tears ran down his cheeks. Bill Tank died four months later of a broken heart in January 1981 in Sheboygan's Memorial Hospital. He had lost the love of his life.

CHAPTER 2:

Who am I?

"Knowledge in youth is wisdom in age."

– English proverb

Dear Lydia:

The more I have thought about writing this book with words of advice to my grandchildren, and I have given it a lot of thought, the more I think this book might be about who I am rather than who you are and who you will become. I am most thankful for the strong foundation of love that I was given growing up. Your Great-Grandmother Lydia Tank was all about connecting with people and especially with little kids. Lydia and Bill gave me that foundation. While I did not know it at the time, one thing I learned over the years as a high school history teacher was that it's often not how intelligent children are when they come to school that matters. A more important determining factor of future success is that emotional foundation they possess as they go out into the world. Because my parents died so young, they will never know how fortunate I feel that I was given that foundation early in my life. Because of that, all I can really do is pay it forward to you, and someday you can pay that same solid foundation forward to your children. Lydia, that's what life is all about.

Although neither of my parents graduated from high school at Sheboygan Central High School or Kohler High School (not uncommon during the Great Depression), growing up I always felt like education was important. For some reason, I was the only one of the four boys in my family projected to go to college. While I did not necessarily think I was any smarter than anyone else, grades and academic achievement were very important to me. I was a pleaser, and I received all the accolades for getting good grades in school. For this reason, I always felt like I could achieve anything I set my mind to.

I acquired my love of reading from your Great-Grandma Lydia Tank. She loved to read, and early on so did I. My dad was not much of a reader, but he liked to build things. As a boy, I often went with him to the local Richardson Brothers lumberyard to buy some wood for building cabinets in our basement. Behind our house there was a heavily wooded area with a creek running through it, which ran into a water-filled abandoned rock quarry (in which I once came extremely close to drowning) known as the "Gulley." It was an adventure playground for young boys, and I feel very fortunate to have had it. As a young boy, I often played army there with friends. We also built tree forts there, which became favorite reading spots. Starting in about fifth grade, I got hooked on reading the Tom Swift adventure stories before progressing to the Hardy Boys series and the Chip Hilton sports books.

As I explored the wonderful world of books throughout fifth grade, I decided that I wanted to become a writer. I proceeded to work on my own adventure series. My parents encouraged me as did my fifth grade teacher, Mrs. Gretchen Hunrath. I was determined. After completing a handwritten story in pencil, I wondered what my next step toward publication was. Somehow, I heard that someone in the wealthy Kohler family had written and published a book. So, without further delay, I rode my bike to the Kohler mansion with my manuscript in hand and knocked on the door. I do not recall if it was Mrs. Kohler or one of their butlers who answered the door, but I was very graciously allowed to enter their home and explain my project. I also do not recall what Mrs. Kohler said, but I know that the visit was quite brief. I also remember that it was very kind of her to allow a young boy into her home and encourage his dream. I was never crushed when the story wasn't published. I moved on quickly. Little did I know that I would write and publish my first book, *Coaching Our Sons*, forty years later.

While we did not have much extra family money, playing sports was cheap entertainment at the time. It was a different era. There were no club teams or AAU traveling teams or high school summer league teams, which kids were pressured to join. As a kid in the blue-collar town of Sheboygan Falls, my neighborhood friends and I would get together and play pick-up baseball games in the street (often dodging cars) during the summer, often challenging a rival neighborhood to a hard-fought game. I spent hours throwing a rubber ball against the side of the garage pretending I was one of the early Milwaukee Brewers. (Not far away from where I was attempting to throw the ball was a small window on the garage. One time I accidentally missed my spot and smashed the window. I dreaded telling my dad. To his great credit as a father, he never said a word. He simply replaced the window.) During the fall, we played football. (I was tall, fast, and could catch well but felt like I only weighed about twenty pounds, so I never enjoyed getting tackled.) Basketball was always my favorite sport. I think I enjoyed it because it was the one sport I could improve at the most by practicing alone.

But it was in junior high school and high school where I discovered sports. My first basketball court was a dirt court on the side of our garage, which served as my mom's laundry line area. My thinking was that I could practice my shooting and pretend I was getting fouled by the clothesline. I guess she wasn't very thrilled with that idea.

Several things came together for me during those early teen years. Now, remember that this was a time of great stress in my family. Your great-grandmother's illness was kicking in, and doctors at the time were not sure how to treat it. Various medications were tried but only seemed to make it worse. Because of mounting medical bills, we lost my parents' dream home and were forced to move into a hundred-year-old house which needed major work. Seeing your mom being taken out of your house during the middle of the night by ambulance, or seeing her being taken to a hospital hundreds of miles away in Rochester, Minnesota without knowing if she will return affected me. I think I was forced to grow up quickly.

I became driven. In basketball, I started to shoot. I wanted to be good, so I shot and shot and shot. I also became more organized. By choosing twelve different spots on my dirt court and wooden backboard, I shot fifty shots per day at each spot—six hundred shots each day. I also bought a notebook and wrote down how many shots I made from each spot on the court. Our local high school program, under the guidance of Wisconsin Hall of Fame Coach Arden Luker, sponsored a free throw shooting contest for junior high kids as well. Several hundred kids participated, and the two best kids were asked to come back and compete against each other at halftime of a varsity game. By making eighteen out of twenty-five, I was one of the two finalists. In the end, I took second place but got a nice trophy. I was so proud. Basketball was quickly becoming my passion and a major part of who I was.

Lydia, the high school years can be difficult for anyone. Don't worry; they go by quickly! For me, basketball was still very important. Although I didn't realize it, I was fortunate to play during the four best years in my high school's history. We won four state championships in three different sports, two of which were in basketball, during my junior and senior years. That was the good news. The bad news was that we had some very talented competition on those teams which made it difficult to get as much playing time as I would have liked. Not always playing was not easy. At one point, I was crushed when I realized that I was not going to be an NBA star. It seemed so unfair to me, but the experience of playing on two state basketball championship teams was beyond awesome to me.

At the same time, I somehow knew that it was not very smart to put all my eggs in the sports basket, so to speak. I understood that going to college and getting an education was going to be my ticket in life, and it was. As I said, I was a pleaser. During my younger years, I think I was fine with being a solid B student. Early in high school, however, something clicked in me, and the drive I had in basketball now carried over into academics. I wanted As badly and wanted to learn as much as I could. Social studies courses had always come easily to me, and history especially opened new worlds to me. I started reading books from the local library about the Civil War. By my later high school years, I was buying my own Civil War books at the Walden Booksellers in Sheboygan, which sadly no longer exists. I read voraciously. Before I graduated, I had read at least a hundred

Civil War related books. Historian Bruce Catton was especially highly regarded. I'm not sure that my high school history teacher was all that thrilled by the fact that one of his students knew so much and could discuss the facts of the Battle of Chancellorsville or the merits of General Robert E. Lee vs. General Ulysses S. Grant intelligently. I had good teachers at Sheboygan Falls High School. I was just driven to know more.

Also during my high school years, I discovered that I liked girls, but I was terribly shy. Being raised in a family of four boys with no girls, I knew absolutely nothing about girls. (Great-Grandma Lydia Tank, who wanted a daughter in the worst way, was known for saying that she felt like a maid in a guy's college dorm. You don't know how many times during your early life I looked at you and thought nostalgically of her.) So many girls were good-looking and beyond anyone I could ever hope for. Shortly after getting my driver's license in 1972, I called a girl on the phone (yes, a landline) who I had seen in one of my classes to ask her to go with me to a movie. I was so scared. Girls were a total mystery to me. I was probably hyperventilating as I dialed her number. She was very cute and a year younger than I was. To my surprise, she said yes. After picking her up at her house in my dad's car, we went to the movie and afterward got something to eat. It was a bad date. I think I said two words the entire time. I was too nervous. As I took her home, I knew I had blown it. I was just so shy! I think she was out of the car before it had stopped moving in her driveway. I also think we both mumbled something like, "See you later." It was a disaster. I felt like a loser. More advice on relationships later.

CHAPTER 3:
The First Time I Held You

"Children are poor men's riches."

– English proverb

Dear Lydia:

Before you were born in the small town of Dodgeville, we called you the "celebrity baby." Having taught in the high school for almost three decades and now with your mom teaching in the elementary school following an All-American career in track and field, I seemed to know everyone. Throughout the last month before your due date your mom had gotten very big, and most people thought you would be born at any time. Many said they were sure you would be born early. I was asked multiple times a day if there was any news yet. I could only shake my head and say, "Nope, none yet. I guess he or she is just not ready to be born yet." (Your mom and dad chose not to know if you were a boy or girl before your birth.)

Everyone was anxious as your May due date came and went. Ten days after your due date, your mom's doctor had a prior engagement out of town over the weekend, so she was determined to induce labor if you reached two weeks past your due date. This proved to be very fortunate, as your parents had the highest confidence in her as an ob-gyn.

So Tuesday, May 17, arrived. It was a very nice spring day in southwestern Wisconsin. As I walked to school in high spirits, I knew that this was "D-Day." You were going to be born today. Throughout the day I got brief updates from your Grandma Becky, who said she did not want to linger near your delivery room, that things seemed to be progressing well, and there was hope that you might arrive in the world by late afternoon. As I walked the five blocks or so from school to our house, I was stopped by three separate people asking if I had heard anything yet. I said no, but I remember thinking that yes, you really are the "celebrity baby," and I was excited to meet you. Even your Aunt Alli, your mom's close sister and best friend who was teaching in Prairie du Chien an hour away, had her friends asking her.

By 4 p.m. your Grandma Becky told me that your mom was close to delivering you. The excitement was building. I remember thinking that this is it. Your Grandma Diane and Grandpa Scott Alleman had also arrived, but all of us wanted your mom and dad to share this special moment together. I told your mom that I would wait at home but to call me as soon as she knew anything. I was prepared to go at any time, and then as late afternoon elapsed into evening ... nothing happened.

I have taught history for many years, and I have always talked about leading causes of death as well as longevity during different time periods in history. For instance, a hundred years ago the average lifespan for Americans was only fifty years. Marriages often did not last as long because people did not live as long. Well into the 1800s in the United States the two leading causes of death were smallpox and childbirth. Even when I was born prematurely at seven months in 1956, survival could be touch and go. But by 2016 in the United States with the great advances in modern medicine, I was most confident that the chance of this happening had dropped dramatically.

By 9 p.m. and still no word of the baby, I called your Grandma Becky, who was praying in the waiting room, and told her that I was going to sleep at home but to call and wake me if you were born soon. I was awakened less than two hours later, but there was an odd sound to Grandma Becky's voice. She said you were born, but she had not seen you yet. As I bolted out of bed, I told her I would be right there. When I got to the maternity waiting area, however, there was a cloudy, surreal atmosphere surrounding everyone. While no one seemed joyous as I had anticipated they would be, all anyone could say was that a baby had been born, and it was a very difficult birth. People looked concerned, yet no one seemed to know much. Other doctors had arrived to assist in your delivery.

Very soon after arriving, your dad came out to talk to us. Now Greg Alleman is a guy who does not startle easily, and he was aware of the gravity of the situation of which his role was to soothe and comfort your mother during your birth. During the final moments before your birth, you got stuck in the birth canal. While your head had emerged, the doctor had difficulty with your shoulder. Luckily you had an excellent doctor and nurses working with your mother and you. Even so, your dad was not sure that either you or your mom were going to make it. When he emerged just minutes after you were born, he looked pretty shook up. He said that you were a girl, you were alive, and that you were big at 10 pounds 15 ounces. While all of us were very excited at your birth and could not wait to see you, one thing I remember the most about the moment was seeing the look of pure joy on your Aunt Alli's face as she thrillingly exclaimed, "It's a girl!" However, it was the doctor's wish that we delay seeing you and your mom until the next day.

The following morning, I had an early eye doctor appointment in Madison, so I could not come to the hospital quite as early as I would have liked. By mid-morning, however, I was on my way back to Dodgeville, and as I got closer the gravity of the situation hit me, and I was overcome with emotion. As I headed directly to the hospital, tears streamed down my cheeks. I do not even remember wondering what your name would be. I went directly to your room, and as I held you in my arms for the first time, your mom introduced me to you as Lydia Jeanne Alleman.

As I sat in the rocking chair holding you in my arms, I spoke softly to you. You were awake and not crying. I wanted you to get to know my voice early on in your life. I told you that you were a very special little girl named after your two great-grandmothers. I also whispered to you that I loved you very much and that I would always be your friend. This is something I have repeatedly said to you throughout your early months, and I mean it. I will always love you, and I will always be your friend.

Letters to Lydia

CHAPTER 4:
What Was Your Mom Like?

"May the hinges of our friendship never grow rusty."

– Irish blessing

Dear Lydia:

Your mom, Ann, was born during an unstable time in our lives. Grandma Becky and I had just sold our house in Alliance, Nebraska, after deciding to move back to Wisconsin. Although we had two young children, Uncle Wes and Aunt Alli, she and I had both quit our jobs to move back and be closer to our families. As we made the move, she told me that she was pregnant with our third child, your mom. After we both got jobs later that summer in Fond du Lac, Wisconsin, we downsized from owning a beautiful four-bedroom home in Nebraska to renting a cramped two-bedroom townhouse in Fond du Lac. I had taken a $10,000 a year cut in pay by going to teach and coach basketball in a private school, but I was happy that I had a job. It was during that year spent in Fond du Lac that your mom was born (yes, all three children slept in one bedroom).

As a young girl, several things stood out about your mom. First, Ann was very easygoing. Nothing bothered her very much. She was drama free. I was always the shopper in the family, and if Grandma Becky had to work on a Saturday, I would take all three kids to Madison for a trip to West Towne Mall. Of course, the toy store was all our kids' favorite stop there, and it was rare that they did not want something. If I told Ann, however, that we were a little tight on money that week and we could not buy anything, she was always calm about it and accepted the fact easily even though I knew there was something she had her eye on. That said, if we went to a bookstore, which was often, we never said no to a book of their choice. Reading was a priority in our family. Your mom and dad seem to be raising you with similar priorities.

From the time Ann was a young girl growing up in Dodgeville, one of her longtime best friends was Lauren Hawkinson, who reminisced about their early days together. "We would go to the high school basketball games and dance when the band played while being more interested in our coloring books and the band than in the games. We would tear up our programs so when the Dodgers won we could throw confetti up in the air." Lauren too had thoughts about Ann's ability to keep things in perspective and her emotions in check. "When I interviewed for the job at the University of Wisconsin, one of the questions they asked me was, 'How do you handle being yelled at?' I thought back to high school basketball. It was halftime of a game, and we were sitting in the locker room with Ann. Coach Busch was mad and yelling at us. As he yelled, a few of us may have started to giggle. He threw the whiteboard marker, and it exploded all over Ann's white warmup pants. She didn't say much but was like, 'Whatever.' If Ann was ever bothered by the yelling, she never showed it. She was always very even-keeled, and I think that helped our team and me. She was a leader on the team."

The second quality which stood out very early on was her intense competitiveness. She did not like to lose at anything, and she did not handle it well if she did. It did not matter if she was competing against boys or girls. Ann wanted to win. Ann's early girlhood years were during my first years as the head boys basketball coach in Dodgeville, and Ann grew up loving basketball. We had great success during those years, winning championships in front of jam-packed gymnasium crowds, and going to two state tournaments during the 1990s and a third in 2004 when she was in middle school, along with narrow misses a few other years. They were golden years for Dodgeville basketball. As a young girl, Ann witnessed it, and it helped mold her. When the five of us in our family drove to distant ocean summer vacation resorts, we invented the "basketball game" to help pass the time in the car. The five of us divided into two teams, and whenever someone was the first to spot a basketball hoop either in someone's driveway, playground, or yard, their team got the point. (It was most fun driving across Indiana, arguably the basketball capital of America.) Your mom, the youngest one, was accused by her brother or sister of cheating, saying that she had seen a basketball hoop across some distant cornfield which no one else had seen. She did not like that and would often tear up at the accusation. I think that she simply wanted to win so badly. She saw the importance of winning. It was in her blood, and her competitive fires burned deeply. When going to basketball camps or playing with other Dodgeville girls at area tournaments, opponents, when sizing up the Dodgeville girls, often pointed out your mom and said, "That's Ann Tank. She's good."

Although Ann was a four-year starter and leading scorer on her high school varsity girls basketball team, something changed for her. While she always kept her passion for basketball and would coach the sport at the middle school level with me, running became her dominant sport. When your mom was in fifth grade, students were required to run a timed mile race, and she was determined to win it. So the night before the event she practiced by running laps around the outside of our house. But after her middle school track career was completed with Ann not losing an event, she walked off the track for the final time and expressed her distaste by saying that she would never run track again. At the time, she saw herself as a basketball player who just did not enjoy running. (More later about the stubborn streak that runs through the family.)

Your Uncle Wes is six years older than your mom and offered good insights into his younger sister and what it means to grow up being a Tank. A talented and well-respected Milwaukee filmmaker and musician, your Uncle Wes noted that there was a natural dichotomy existing within your mom. "She presents the appearance of being kind and sweet to everyone, even the people she's not that fond of, but on the other hand, she is always a ferocious competitor." Ann was never involved in anything simply for the social aspect. She was always there to win.

Another aspect of your mom as noted by your Uncle Wes was that being a Tank often meant involving yourself in a certain goal-oriented lifestyle. Achieving goals was always a priority. He is right. As Wes stated, "Not everyone understands this. Some people admire this, but others are turned off by it. There seems to be an internal drive to achieve, not waste time, and be productive." I see this too in all three of my children.

Shortly before graduating from UW-Platteville, your dad was to receive an award from the Math Department there. His parents, Diane and Scott, and grandparents, Papa D and Jeanne, drove several hours to witness the occasion. After they parked their car and entered the university building, they all had to use the restroom after the long trip. As Papa D later related, "As we went down the hall, I noticed a nice-looking girl waiting by the steps. I thought to myself, 'I hope Greg's girlfriend is going to look like her.' After everyone came out of the restroom, Greg said, 'I will take you to meet Ann now,' and he took me right over to that girl." Obviously, he could not have been happier for his grandson.

CHAPTER 5:
What Was Your Dad Like?

*"Never say never, because limits, like fears,
are often just an illusion."*

– Michael Jordan

Dear Lydia:

Your mother didn't date much in middle or high school. She was involved in basketball and running, and at least outwardly she didn't show much interest in boys or dating. When the topic later came up well after college, both your mom and Aunt Alli said, "Well, no boys would ask us out because of you, Dad." My response was, "Okay, so what's your point?" They said that guys were afraid of me. Even when your mom and Aunt Alli went off to college in Platteville, only thirty minutes down the road, they said that some guys feared me. I guess I didn't see that or was oblivious to it. Anyway, I am glad that your dad had the courage to ask your mom out and then the courage to ask her to marry him, despite her father.

Your dad was born in Spring Valley, Illinois, the second of four children to Scott and Diane Alleman of Granville, Illinois, a small agricultural community in central Illinois less than an hour from Peoria or Bloomington. His siblings are your Uncle Doug, Uncle Kevin, and Aunt Katie. Your Grandpa Scott is retired from the State of Illinois Highway Department, where he worked for many years, and your Grandma Diane teaches kindergarten in the Granville School District.

While your dad grew up in Granville very close to and admiring his brother Doug, who was two and a half years older than him, Grandpa Scott and Grandma Diane could quickly see differences between the two boys. Said your Grandma Diane, "Douglas and Gregory were different. Douglas came out fighting. Gregory always seemed to sit back and watch." If there were ever any controversy or potential consequences, "Doug would admit to nothing. Greg would apologize, and that would be it. Douglas and I were two happy semis coming at each other."

Besides sports, as a boy your dad spent hours occupied in Granville by two things: Legos and Teenage Mutant Ninja Turtles. Your Grandpa Scott said, "Gregory was always into Legos and Ninja Turtles. He was so easy to buy gifts for. He was so into it that it was hard to stop." Said Grandma Diane, "When Greg was about two and a half years old, we bought Douglas a Ninja Turtle as a gift, and Gregory went along when we picked it out. I told him, 'Don't tell Douglas! Don't tell Douglas!' Of course, Gregory said, 'I won't tell. I won't tell.' When Doug came home from school that day, he barely got his feet off the bus, and Greg was so excited he yelled, 'We got you a Ninja Turtle!' "

When your dad started attending Granville Middle School along with his friends, life for him was good. His mother, though, at times thought things might be too good for her second son. "Everybody really liked him. If he wanted to become class president, then he would become the class president. I worried a little bit. In high school, he ran for something, and I was so glad when he didn't get it. He just needed to see that things are not always handed to you. When it happened, he wasn't even upset. He was like, 'Hmmm, this is different.'" Not unusually, it was during your dad's middle school years that he discovered girls nearly by accident. In her own words, Grandma Diane was "pretty strict" with raising her four children, Greg included, but she allowed your dad to attend his first dance at the local YMCA when he was in sixth grade. Later, she ran into the mother of a sixth grade girl who relayed some inside information that Greg and her daughter had kissed while at the dance. Your Grandma Diane said, "I thought this was very wrong, but we didn't know how to tell him, but it's wrong! It was tricky. He is very sensitive, and we knew he would take it to heart. I asked him, 'Did you and Emily kiss?' He said, 'Once.' I said that I was sorry that I put him in a spot he wasn't ready to handle. 'Maybe we won't go back to any more Y dances.' " In your dad's defense, he did say, "I didn't even want to, and I had no intention. I guess it was peer pressure."

While a member of the cross country and track teams at UW-Platteville, your mom met Greg Alleman. Very quickly his good personal qualities became apparent. Your Grandpa Scott and Grandma Diane reflect and perhaps see two positive things about Greg that stand above the others. When asked what made his son special, the first thing Grandpa Scott said was, "He was so focused. Things never bothered him. He could handle adversity and not crumble." Your Grandma Diane, meanwhile, saw a different side of her son, saying, "Gregory was born good. Scott is too. He is good to the bone. I'm a good person. My other three kids are great people. I'm kind, but Greg and Scott take it to a higher level. My dad was that way. For example, Greg will not get Ann a pair of pants for their anniversary. He will focus on what is really meaningful to her."

Lydia, your dad was someone who could differentiate between doing what he thought was right and what was wrong. As a five-year-old, Greg gave advice to his mother. According to Grandma Diane, "I was pregnant with Kevin and went to the doctor's office to get some blood drawn. I couldn't watch them do it, but Greg was so focused on it. Afterward, we stopped at McDonald's because I really wanted a diet soda. As we drove into the McDonald's parking lot, Greg said, 'Mom, didn't the doctor say that soda was not good for the baby?' Of course, I didn't have that soda."

Religion and a strong faith in God have always been important to your father. From an early age in Granville, your dad could connect with his spirituality. Grandma Diane stated, "We went to church every Sunday, and like his older brother Doug, he was an altar boy. Doug had been the leader of the altar boys, and then so was Greg."

There were times, however, when all the two brothers had to do was look at each other the wrong way during the church service. Grandma Diane squirmed in her seat as she glared at her two boys as if to scream, "Stop it!" which she was unable to do at the time, but was addressed on the way home after the service. Grandpa Scott also noted that one of the Catholic priests had a positive effect on your dad. "One father was very good. Father Kruse made it fun for the kids. He really got into it with them. He was very good and has now moved up at the diocese."

There is a strong religious influence that runs in the family. According to Grandma Diane, "A lot of the religion also came from my folks. My dad had two sisters who became nuns and an uncle who was a priest. For a time, we thought Gregory might become a priest." Your mom interjected, "I put the kibosh to that idea!"

Lydia, while talking about your dad, I must tell you about your dad's grandfather, Darrell Alleman. Papa D was born on the eve of the Great Depression in 1929 in Tonica, Illinois. His family lost their farmland during the Great Depression and were forced to move to rural McNabb, Illinois, where he went to a one-room country school until eighth grade and met your Great-Grandma Jeanne (Anderson) Alleman. Because of where the family farm was located, Papa D went to Hopkins High School in Granville. As tragic as it was to lose the family farm, Papa D understood that it wasn't too bad because without that happening, he would never have met the love of his life.

CHAPTER 6:
Tank Humor

> Teacher: *"General William Hull was a famous US War of 1812 commander."*
> Student: *"Why do we have to know about him?"*
> Teacher: *"Just for the hull of it."*
>
> – Chuck Tank

Dear Lydia:

One reason that I so wish you could have known Bill Tank was his incredible sense of humor. He could make people laugh, which is a true gift. Growing up in Sheboygan Falls, I had five girl cousins, daughters of my mom's sister Hilda Heule, who were all roughly the same ages as my brothers and me. For years after my parents were gone, whenever I would get together with them they always spoke of my dad's ability to tease them. Two of his tricks stood out. The first was whenever one of the cousins would go and kiss him goodbye, he would stick out his false teeth at the last second. Of course, they'd all go "Eww!" whenever he did that.

Around 1969 or 1970 my dad, who had walked with a limp for as long as I could remember (saying it was the result of an old war wound, which was not true), received one of the first total hip replacement surgeries done in the Sheboygan area. Following this, he required the use of a cane to walk. No big deal except for the fact that he became known for sticking that cane out to trip you whenever you walked by. Of course, because everything my dad did or said was done with a deadpan straight face, it was nearly impossible to know if he was joking or not. Some would say that you could only believe about 10 percent of anything my dad said, but you never knew which 10 percent it was. One thing I remember my dad jokingly said a lot was, "You will miss me when I'm gone!" Now I understand how prophetic he really was.

As a high school history teacher for thirty-eight years and still going, I have come to understand that teachers teach what they know and who they are. Because of this, I always try to use Tank humor in my classroom, and I have discovered that the best jokes are the ones that make fun of myself rather than others. Like my dad, I try to keep a straight face whenever I say something that I think is funny. Kids have said, though, that my mouth curves upward if I'm pausing for them to laugh. If they don't laugh, or if they simply groan loudly, I most often respond by jokingly saying things like, "You know my self-esteem can only take so much!" or "If I want abuse like this, I can go home!"

Classic Chuck Tank historical humor. (Someday this will become a thing of the past!):

- Student: "My grandfather fought in a tank during World War II."
  Teacher: "My dad was a Tank during World War II."

- "During the American Revolution, the United States received much needed help in their quest for victory from the French, especially the use of the French navy. The leading French naval commander was Admiral de Grasse. Of course, the British hated him. Throughout the war the British always said how they wanted to cut de Grasse … (pause for dramatic effect). They wanted to mow him down and trim back his sails in their search for victory."

- "During World War I, the Great War in which nine million people sacrificed their lives, one of the worst battles was at the French town of Verdun. Several hundred thousand soldiers died there. When it was over, neither side won or lost. They simply said, 'That's it, Verdun.'"

- "At the end of the nineteenth century as imperialism was at its peak in areas such as China, factions developed which opposed foreigners in their countries. In China, it was a radical group called the Boxers who demanded that foreigners leave." I would then say, "The Boxer Rebellion was a rather brief event. Many people, literally thongs of people, opposed American influence."

- Growing up with the last name Tank, I had many people ask me, "Did you have an Uncle Sherman?" My response, as I shrugged and laughed it off for the hundredth time, became, "No, but I did have an Uncle Septic."

As a dad and like my dad, I have always been a tease, and I get a great thrill from scaring people. When your mom turned thirteen on New Year's Eve 2002, we hosted a small birthday party for her here at our home. Six of Ann's friends were invited over for dinner, cake, and a sleepover. Your Grandma Becky and I wondered what we could do for thirteen-year-old girls that would be fun for them. We decided to take the eight of them, including your mom and Aunt Alli, to the high school at night to play hide-and-go-seek. It was so fun. At the time there were no security cameras, and the only light came from the red glow of the exit signs lighting the hallways. The rule was that anyone could hide anywhere in the dark building except the locker room area or back hallway, and all classrooms except mine were locked. The girls had so much fun. The highlight of the night was when I was the last to be found. I hid at the entrance to my office. It was dark with only an eerie red glow from the exit signs. They didn't know it, but I had brought a "Scream" mask along. I heard them asking each other, "Do you know where he is?" As they slowly walked toward me in the semi-darkness, I kneeled. When the first one spotted me, I stood up as they screamed together. For years they talked about how fun Ann's thirteenth birthday party was.

Your Grandma Becky said that she loved how I could always make her laugh. Well, maybe not always. Tank humor came through in me whenever someone would come last out of the house, and I would blast the car horn and then laugh hysterically as they got mad at me. Or as we're driving down the highway, anyone sitting in the passenger seat could never have their arm hanging out the window because I would roll it up from the driver's side. (I could always get your Uncle Wes on that one!) Perhaps my favorite was when your Grandma Becky was busy preparing one of her great meals and was standing in the kitchen over the sink. Without her knowing, I would sneak outside, go up to that window, and smush my face up against the glass and stay there until she looked up. Once she saw me, she would scream and of course, I would laugh and laugh.

PART 2:
Things to Consider as You Go Through Life

CHAPTER 7:
The Important Things

"Only those who dare to fail greatly can ever achieve greatly."

– Robert F. Kennedy

Dear Lydia:

When the idea to write a book of advice to my grandchildren came to me as I was walking the streets of Dodgeville on a cold Wisconsin winter evening, the thoughts and opinions in this chapter were the first things to come to my mind. They could be the difference makers in your life. I hope that I might share a few thoughts with you here, which at age sixteen you may not see as important at all, but at age twenty-five or thirty, you may see as great advice. For me at age sixty, they are things of importance that I see in my life.

First of all, at some point in your life you will see the big picture. I like to say that life can be like a thousand-piece jigsaw puzzle in which all your daily events, feelings and emotions, and everyone you interact with are all the various pieces of that puzzle. You see them but may or may not see how they all connect. Together they add up to the person you have become. Then at some point, things just seem to come together, and suddenly you get it. You don't just see those individual pieces, but instead, you can visualize the big picture of life. Once that happens, most other decisions in your life seem to fall into place. Maybe it's just maturity. I'm not sure. Just know that it will happen. Try to make it happen sooner rather than later. Along with that, sometimes there is a tendency to spend so much time and energy on things that are not very important. I think it is an important skill to be able to make those decisions quickly and then move on without regret. I have seen so many people become practically paralyzed by the inability to make little choices.

Every day in your early life you are being shaped. Give some thought to the kind of person you want to be. As you grow older, many people will naturally ask you what you want to be when you grow up. There's nothing wrong with that, and I am sure you will have your mind set on various things throughout the years before changing it. One piece of advice, which I believe may be even more important though, is the understanding that the kind of person you are is far more important than your achievements, what you do, the awards you earn, or even how you look. Think about that the next time you just have to get that new dress to impress all of your friends. Those things go on in school every day. Personally, I think the greatest compliment anyone can give you is when you are not present, and your name is brought up, and someone else simply says, "Lydia Alleman is such a nice person." I'll have more to say about this in a different chapter.

While I do not think that the pursuit of money and material things like clothes, cars, or stuff are most important, and their accumulation will not make you a happy person, I do believe that good things in life rarely just happen. (No, I have never bought a lottery ticket and never will.) I have always been a goal-oriented guy. Set your goal and then work harder than anyone else. I believe that you must work hard to achieve the things that are most important to you. In other words, you must earn it. It won't just happen. An important consequence of that, however, is how you handle adversity. This has the potential to define you. As I said earlier, your Great-Grandmother Lydia Tank was a woman children were drawn to and many people seemed to like, but it was how she handled adversity in her own life which made her stand above the rest.

As you go through life, don't hurry. So many people make the mistake of thinking that if they are always busy, they are more productive and perhaps a better person. I think this is wrong. I have always liked the saying, "Take your time. Think a lot." It's important to think things through. Ask many questions. Know that it is rare that someone else has not been in the same situation you are in. Understand their perspective. Today people make the mistake of thinking their way is the only way.

Take notes on things. I recommend that you keep a notebook and that you take it with you wherever you go. Refer to it at various times. This was something I learned during my years as a varsity basketball coach, but I have carried it over into my teaching career. Use it as a learning tool. You will learn something every day. Be aware of what you are learning. Write it down! Keep lists or even notebooks. Ask yourself how you learn best. Do you learn best from books like I do? Do you learn best from interacting with people? Do you learn best online? Do you have a favorite place in which you learn, or a best time of the day, or even a best day of the week? These are things you should think about as you get older. Once you figure out some of these things, you will better understand who you are as a person.

The last piece of advice I would like to give you regarding this broad topic relates to the fact that I am a thinker. (Your Grandma Becky sometimes tells me that I think too much, and she is likely correct on that one!) My advice to you is that if something is bothering you, Lydia, understand that things will look different tomorrow. Don't make quick, impulsive decisions, which are almost always wrong. Think about it. Talk to people whose advice you value. Think some more. Then make your decision. You won't regret it.

CHAPTER 8:
Finding Your Passion in Life

"The biggest adventure you can ever take is to live the life of your dreams."

– Oprah Winfrey

Dear Lydia:

Finding your passion in life is discovering your purpose, why you are here. This is a gift. I believe that everyone has a purpose, a reason for living. Yet many people never know what their purpose is. Instead, they live their daily lives by getting up, going to school or work, eating meals, and performing all the basics of life without discovering what their true passion is. To me this is sad. My advice to you is to give this some thought, and over time the light bulb will go on.

This idea of finding your passion sounds good on paper, but it's not always so easy. How do you figure out what your passion is? In a speech I give to high school students, I talk to them about the importance of finding their passion. A sixteen-year-old girl in my US history class, who seemed very motivated in school and was driven to be successful, raised her hand and asked me with true concern, "What if I don't know what my passion is?" My answer to her was your passion fits your dreams. If you could be or have anything, what would it be? I also said that you know it's your passion when you find yourself daydreaming about it while you're doing something else. So, Lydia, identify your dream.

Once you decide to pursue your passion, you will need to commit yourself. You must develop a "find a way" attitude. In my thirty-eight years of teaching, I have heard many students talk a good game, but when it came down to it, they weren't willing to work hard enough to achieve what they said they wanted. They most often found an excuse or someone else to blame for their weakness or failure. When they chose the easy path, often their friends or parents were the first ones to support them and say it was okay. Avoid this at all costs!

Throughout your life, you will hear a lot about the value of having a strong work ethic. Kids are raised on this, especially here in Wisconsin and the Midwest. I have already told you about how hard my parents, as children of the Great Depression, worked without complaint to provide for our family. It was just expected. That always impressed me. For you, understand that hard work and talent can take you to the top 3 percent, but at some point, you have to find a way to go above and beyond. For instance, many students say that they want to get an A in a difficult class, but are you willing to get out of bed an hour earlier than you normally would for weeks to study for a test? Are you willing to run ten more miles than anyone else after you have already completed your intense weekly workouts? Are you willing to shoot a hundred extra three-point shots on a hot July day even after you've already shot five hundred and your friends are going swimming and urging you to come along? Most kids say they are committed, but only a few are willing to "walk the talk." If you want to achieve your dream, walk the talk.

Be careful. I tell you to take your time and think things through because there is a fine line between a hobby and a passion or a passion and an obsession. In other words, something very positive can become a negative quickly. Don't become obsessed. For years during my early teens, my dream was to become an NBA star like my idol, Jerry West. I did everything I could to emulate him, yet it still did not happen. I was pretty upset about it for a while. So, what did I do instead? I went on to become a successful high school basketball coach.

Also, there comes a time to let go. When do you know? All I can say is when that time comes, you will know. It also helps to find someone who shares your passion and supports you. For instance, your mom and Aunt Alli had each other to lean on. Their bond as sisters and their passion for running grew strong over the years. When you find that person, together you can celebrate your victories.

Lydia, I hope that you can discover your passion, and even if it may change over time (it almost always does change, often more than once), you have great potential to achieve anything you desire. (Today, I can say without hesitation that at the great age of one year and four months, your passion in life is dogs. Anytime you see a dog you say, "Dog, dog, dog!" and you have to go and see and talk to it. I love seeing how passionate you are about dogs!)

CHAPTER 9:
Setting Goals and Chasing Your Dreams

"The man who removes a mountain begins by carrying away small stones."

– Chinese proverb

Dear Lydia:

One of the rules I have lived by since I was a boy is that great things rarely just happen. Because of that, I have always been a goal-oriented person. I think about want I want to achieve, and I go after it. When I was young and wanted to pursue my dream of becoming a basketball star, I decided that the best way for me to do that was to shoot more daily shots than anyone else. I started shooting six hundred shots a day (fifty from twelve spots on the basketball court) and kept a record in a notebook of how many I made from each spot. My goal was always a very difficult 80 percent, and I got angry at myself if I did not make it especially when shooting what today would be three-point shots. Every day during the hot Wisconsin summer months I shot and shot and shot. By the time I was in high school, I was proud that my Hall of Fame high school coach Arden Luker called me the best shooter on the team.

Many kids who grow up with little money see sports as their ticket to the good life, and they set that goal of becoming a pro, even during the late 1960s and early 1970s before the days of the massive contracts. Yes, that was my dream. It was more than that, though. I also somehow saw early, as I watched my dad come home from working long hours in the foundry at the Kohler Company, that education was a key to my success. I never thought that I was any smarter than anyone else, but I became driven. I wanted to succeed. High grades and success in school also became very important to me. A common mistake that many students make today is thinking that others get high grades in school because they are smarter or the teacher likes them more. Some students think that they are bad test takers and don't study at all. Lydia, my advice to you is to study, study, study! Tell yourself that while other students may be smarter than you, no one will ever work harder than you.

In recent years, I have given a speech to various groups about what I consider a recipe for success either in academics or athletics. I break down the elements into four separate parts and tell people to write it down on a piece of paper and post it somewhere they will see it every day.

- Dreaming your **dream**: As I said in the last chapter, if you could have or be anything, what would it be? Before you do this, I want to remind you to be somewhat cautious here. Think about it a lot, and get advice from someone you can trust. I say that because you often hear people say, "Dream big!" I'm not so sure that's good advice, and I wonder if you might be setting yourself up for failure. Instead, I would say, "Dream big, but be prepared for obstacles, and at the same time, have a plan B to fall back on."

- Set realistic short-term and long-term **goals** that will steadily take you down the path to making your dream come true. Ask yourself, even if your dream is to become a doctor in ten years, what are some things you can do *today* to help that dream become a reality. Also regarding goal setting, I think the best goals are not for yourself. The best goals are ones in which you do something nice for someone else or try to make someone else happy. Some people will disagree with me on this point. Their goal may be to make a million dollars, which is fine. I just think that you will feel better about yourself if you do things in which you help others, especially those who can never repay you.

- Create a detailed **plan**: The busier I get, I find that writing things down helps me stay focused. I'm a morning person so sometimes as I write down what I need to get done, I write down the time of the day I want to do them. This helps me stay organized during times of stress. If I know I have a lot to do on the weekend, then I plan to do the most during the early morning hours.

- Perhaps most importantly, the fourth part of the process is the ability to **persevere**: Understand that with any dream worth achieving, you will face setbacks. You simply must have the stubborn attitude that you are not going to give up. (Trust me. It's within me. It's within your mom. As of now you are just over one year old, but I see that stubbornness in you. If you don't want to do something, you won't.) I tell this to my Advanced Placement US History students who come into the class either apprehensive of the difficulty of the course or downright afraid. The single greatest factor of their success in the class is their ability to persevere.

Many people today believe they are doing all the things I just suggested to you. Then when they fall short of achieving their dream, they are confused or dismayed and wonder why. Those people are told to do their best, and in their minds they are, but in reality it's not even close. Social media today commands the attention of so many people. (I have sat in staff meetings in which the topic was cell phone usage policy and staff members were on their cell phones.) Check it out some time. You can either watch other people or monitor yourself. How much time do you waste on social media? Here's a piece of advice from a grandfather to his grandchildren: When you're studying or doing homework, don't have your phone or any internet device anywhere in the room unless it's necessary for what you're doing.

Lastly, be sure to set the bar high, and don't fear failure. You have a great support group to catch you if you fall. Then just work harder than anyone else. You can do it!

CHAPTER 10:
Being a Good Person

"Do not judge another until you have walked two moons in his moccasins."

– Native American proverb

Dear Lydia:

One thing I have always wondered is why do people who consistently act like jerks not know that they are jerks? It's true. They just don't get it. No one thinks that they're a jerk. Even bullies have their own reason or excuse for doing whatever mean thing they did. My advice to you is to look at yourself in the mirror and try to be honest with yourself. I guess this is the "treat others how you would like to be treated" chapter. Another way of looking at it is to ask yourself what you would like people to say about you. Would you rather have someone say something like, "She's really pretty," or "She's really smart," or "She's a really good person"? I guess you already know how I would answer that one because I think that being a good person is really what it's all about.

My teaching has evolved after having taught high school history for almost four decades (although my students claim that

I use the same jokes every year). (One thing I tell my students as we fight the Civil War every year in my classroom is that although they may be doubtful early in the war, fear not, the North has come storming back to win every year. Another is that I can never understand why the *Titanic* hits the iceberg every year; they never learn.) I believe that I am a better teacher now than I was even a few years ago. I think I do a better job of reaching out and connecting with all my students. One of my proudest moments as a high school teacher happened this past year when one of my students was at our elementary school picking up some of her siblings when she saw your mom, who teaches physical education there, on bus duty. The student had recently moved to Dodgeville and had just learned by seeing your picture on my desk that your mom was my daughter. The high school girl went up to Ann and asked her, "You're Coach Tank's daughter?" After Ann nodded, the girl said, "He is the nicest person I have ever met." After coaching basketball successfully for thirty years, winning championships, being presented the key to the City of Dodgeville in 1993, and teaching for thirty-eight years, no one has ever paid me a greater compliment.

Lydia, let's talk for a minute about the importance of empathy. Empathy is when you care about others. It is impossible to be a good person if you do not have empathy for others. Imagine how great the world would be if everyone had empathy for everyone else. Empathy is so important. As a teacher, I have come to understand this. There is a saying in education that goes, "Kids don't care how much you know until they know how much you care." This is so true. You come from a family of teachers. Maybe you will teach or maybe not. Whatever you do, empathy for others will be crucial. Please note that it has got to be true empathy and not fake empathy. No one appreciates someone who isn't real with them.

So, how do you know if you are a good person or not? This can be difficult because even good people can make mistakes. For me, I have tried to live my life according to two broad rules which Lydia Tank, the third daughter of German immigrants, taught me during the 1950s and 1960s: Always do your best at whatever you do and always do what is right. As I am now entering my sixties, I cannot tell you how many times during my life I have been confronted with a situation or a task in which I wasn't sure what to do. I referred to those two simple rules, and the answer was most often made clear. To Lydia Tank, I say a big "Thank you!" for that.

I really like the idea of doing something nice for someone else with no strings attached. Wouldn't it be great if you had a ton of money to go around and help people who really need it? Personally, I don't like it when you see someone famous donate to a worthy cause but then stand and pose in front of the cameras for the publicity. It reminds me of two famous New York Yankees of the 1920s and 1930s, Babe Ruth and Lou Gehrig, both future Hall of Fame members of the Yankees' famous Murderers' Row. In my reading, I have learned that Ruth, the famous Sultan of Swat, would go to New York area hospitals and get his picture taken with sick children who idolized him. Of course, the media loved it and would publish the pictures in the newspapers. Lou Gehrig, his more unassuming teammate and famous Iron Horse because he played in more consecutive games than anyone else, would also visit children in hospitals. However, Gehrig would not tell the press, so few people ever knew, and of course, no one took his picture for the papers. To me, he was the better person because he did the good deed without expecting the glory.

Sometimes people want to pay you back if you do something nice for them. That's understandable. I'm the same way. I like the whole concept of paying something forward. A primary reason I am writing this book to my grandchildren is that I feel I owe a debt to my parents who are gone, and I feel like paying this forward to you is the best thing to do.

Lydia, I want to tell you with great confidence that I believe that both your mom and your dad are good people. Everyone has weaknesses, but your parents have very few. I would advise you that if in the future you ask them for advice and they give it to you, listen to them!

Lastly, one thing I have done and would urge you to do is to write down that you want to make someone happy today. When you do that, it makes it more real.

CHAPTER 11:
Honesty

"Corn can't expect justice from a court composed of chickens."

– African proverb

Dear Lydia:

Growing up you may often hear that "honesty is the best policy" like I did. You will be told by your parents and teachers that it's always best to tell the truth. In the last chapter, I spoke to you about the importance of being a good person. Of course, a good person is always truthful, right? Well, maybe. In this chapter I want to talk to you about honesty but especially about the importance of being honest with yourself. In other words, what do you see when you look at yourself in the mirror?

Some people are good liars. I believe that lying and dishonesty might even be a growing trend in our society today. The excuse for lying is that it allows you to achieve whatever you desire. Also, once you tell a lie and get away with it, the easier it is to lie again. Then the more often someone tells the same lie, they actually begin to believe it as truth. Then when those people are confronted and the lie is exposed, they are the ones who act insulted. How dare you call them a liar!

History is full of people who became quite adept at lying or telling half-truths. Early in the Civil War, boys and young men (even a few girls) from the North and the South rushed off to enlist, thinking the war was going to be an adventure that would be over quickly. Little did they know it would become the bloodiest war in American history. The rule in the North was that the young men were required to be eighteen years or older to enlist. Not wanting to get into trouble for lying, some of these young men wrote the number 18 on a small piece of paper and placed it inside their shoe under one of their feet. When it came time for them to sign their name and they were asked, "Are you over 18?" They could truthfully respond by saying, "Yes, I am over 18." I have a difficult time imagining people today facing the same dilemma.

On the other hand, during the 1930s as Adolf Hitler rose to power and became the fascist ruler of Nazi Germany, the demagogue proclaimed that to gain the support of the masses, leaders should not simply tell them small fibs. No, Hitler used what he called the "big lie." Tell people everything he felt they wanted to hear, including gross lies. Because of Hitler's initial successes, people have studied this method of manipulation of people's thinking ever since.

My advice to you, Lydia, is to stay away from people who use the big lie. I understand that sometimes a situation may require you to be less than truthful, but as a general rule, tell the truth. (If Grandma Becky asks me if I like her recent haircut, it's a given that I'm going to say yes. Although, if I don't say anything, and she is forced to ask, I'm already in trouble.) So sometimes it's better to be a little less than truthful. That said, I almost never believe what people tell me if they begin by saying, "I'll be honest...." When I hear that, it makes me wonder if they don't say that, are they not being honest? Another thing to be careful of regarding honesty is the ability to hurt someone's feelings. Sometimes people say something, and then when they're called out for saying it, their response is, "Well, I was just being honest!" or "Well, it's the truth!" (Your Grandma Becky says that I tend to be a little oversensitive). If you know someone whose feelings are easily hurt by the truth, try to filter what you say. You cannot win if you hurt someone's feelings, even if it's true.

Quite often dishonest people are lazy people. They often take the shortcut to gain what they want or to make themselves look good. What I said earlier is especially true here. In life, it really doesn't matter what you do or what your accomplishments are. What matters most is who you are. One reflective thing to do is to keep an honesty journal or diary. Take the time to write in it every day, and be completely honest with yourself. Write down ways in which you were or were not honest that day. Express your feelings. How did you feel about what you said or did, especially if no one was around to hear or see you? Also ask yourself, who is the most honest person you know or have ever met? Who is the most dishonest person you know or have ever met?

Having been a high school history teacher for such a long time, I have developed a keen sense of when someone is telling me the truth, a half-truth, or an outright lie. If someone is lying to you, they often have trouble looking you in the eye, especially if they don't have the habit of lying. For example, when your Uncle Wes was in middle school, he told a little white lie, and I immediately called him out on it, and he quickly fessed up and apologized. When your Grandma Becky asked me how I knew, I explained that I had learned to spot a lie through my years of teaching, and he couldn't look me in the eye.

CHAPTER 12:
Ethics

*"The right way is not always the popular and easy way.
Standing for right when it is unpopular is a
true test of moral character."*

– Margaret Chase Smith

Dear Lydia:

Back in the late 1970s when I was an undergraduate student at UW-Oshkosh, I loved history and was driven to learn it. Even as a freshman there I enjoyed going to the university library and checking out books from their history section. It was like windows in my mind were being opened. I remember sitting and taking notes in Dr. Watson Parker's history classes and being so inspired by him to learn more. I admired him and aspired to be like him. I lived in North Scott Hall, a high-rise coed dormitory famous for its wild and drunken parties and one in which not a lot of studying went on. I was the exception to that rule. Again, I was driven to get the best possible grades. I wanted an A in every class. (I also didn't drink while I was in college, which was rare at UW-Oshkosh, even though the legal drinking age was eighteen at the time.) Another freshman who lived on my floor in the dorm, who was not a history major like

I was but was taking an Introduction to United States History class in one of the three hundred-plus seat lecture pits, had an upcoming test in the class and was worried about how he was going to do. He had not studied. He also knew that I came from a family who had no extra money, while his was well off. He cornered me and quietly offered me $50 to go into that lecture hall and take the exam for him. I remember him quite assuredly telling me that it would be easy. They didn't know who he was and didn't even check ID cards. He even sort of threatened to beat me up if I refused. (I was tall but thin and not ready to fight, and he was bigger than me.) Well, I didn't do it. I felt it was wrong. (I hadn't even thought of the fact that if I was caught, I could be expelled for cheating.) I had made an ethical choice. In this case it was the right choice. Lydia, know that in your life, you will be confronted by ethical choices.

I am sixty years old. I wish that I could tell you that throughout my life I always made the right choice as I did in college when I was faced with an ethical dilemma. It's not that easy. For instance, in 1986 I was a young history teacher and basketball coach in Alliance, Nebraska. My players were talented and seemed to like how I coached them. I did not understand at all that I had a lot to learn as a coach. The year before, my first year as a head varsity coach, we played an eventual state champion from Torrington, Wyoming. They had three players who were between 6'5" and 7' in height. All three went on to play Division I college basketball. My tallest player was at most 6'2". Their team was coached by a man who was famous in the area for winning championships at three different high schools. It was my first year as a varsity head coach, and I think they beat us by about fifty points. What I remember most about that game in our gym though was that with about two minutes to go and the game well in hand, and both teams' starters sitting on the bench, their seven-footer was put back into the game. They ran a play to set him up for a massive dunk against our non-starters before being removed from the game again, leaving our players and fans more than a little upset. There was no rule against doing this; however, I thought it was unethical. Well, fast forward to a year later. All our players were back on our team, while most of theirs had graduated when we went to Torrington to play the return matchup. None of our players or fans had forgotten the beating we had taken a year

Letters to Lydia

earlier. This time the outcome was reversed, and we beat them handily. With less than a minute to go in the game and all of both teams' best players seated on the bench, the score was 99–53 in our favor. Our crowd and team were anxious to go over the 100-point mark. I will never forget my best player sitting next to me looked up at me and said, "Coach, please." So, I did it. Against my better judgment, I put my best player back into the game with twenty seconds left. He got fouled and made both free throws, putting us over the 100-point mark. Some said that their fans were so angry that we were lucky to get back on the bus and make it out of Torrington, Wyoming, on that cold December night. Alliance school administrators received mail from concerned Torrington fans wondering how our school could put our team in my hands. Obviously, I had no ethics. Their collective memory was short as they forgot about the year before. Regardless, as I look back on that incident now many years later, I regret my decision. To be ethical means to do the right thing regardless of outside pressures. What I did was not the right thing to do.

Sometimes I wonder if it's even possible today for politicians to remain ethical. Does anyone do the right thing? During each election cycle, everyone is subjected to a barrage of negative political ads, which either twist and manipulate the truth or lie about a candidate's opponent. Yet it works. People believe those negative ads. I just wonder why anyone would want someone representing them in our democratic government who has used lies and twisted facts to get elected. I am not going to advise you on how to vote politically. I know you will do what you believe is right. The political advice I am going to leave you with is to vote for the first person who wants to help people and is running for office without the help of any negative ads. Of course, then you may never get to cast a ballot in any election.

In some ways, this is why I don't like public relations. Rarely do you get the whole truth. I have always believed that if someone or something is really good, it should speak for itself. (I love the old Green Bay Packer Coach Vince Lombardi saying, "If you are fortunate enough to get into the end zone and score a touchdown, act like you've been there before.") You should not have to promote it.

Similarly, I dread commercials. A commercial wants you to purchase their product. Advertisers attempt to get you to believe that they care about you; they don't. To me, car commercials are the worst. Dealers want you to believe that a certain vehicle is the best one ever made and perfect for you. They schmooze you into believing they care about who you are as they ask about your family. Once you buy the vehicle, however, and want to trade it in, then that car isn't quite so good anymore. Suddenly they find every little fault. I understand that car dealers are just trying to make a dollar, but to me, it's not ethical.

Lastly, regarding ethics, my advice to you is to study great people. Examine what made them great. I believe you will discover that when confronted with an ethical decision, time after time great people have chosen the right path. If you can choose that path in your life even if no one else knows what you did, that's even better.

CHAPTER 13:
Change

*"You're off to great places!
Today is your day!
Your mountain is waiting.
So…get on your way!"*

– Dr. Seuss (Theodore Geisel)

Dear Lydia:

When I was eighteen years old and about to leave Sheboygan Falls and become the first in my family to go to college, my mother, your Great-Grandmother Lydia Tank, someone to whom I was very close, took me aside and gave me a piece of wisdom which I will never forget. Her advice to me was, "Never forget who you are or where you come from." In essence, she was telling me, "Don't change." At the time, I remember thinking that of course I wouldn't change. I was who I was and always would be. Looking back at it now through the lens of time, I think she was expressing a legitimate fear that I would start thinking I was smarter than anyone else or better than anyone else. If I could pass on anything to you, Lydia Alleman, it is this same advice: "Never forget who you are or where you come from."

I believe that life is evolutionary. Everyone changes throughout their lives. You may not realize it at first, but you are not the same person at age twenty that you will be at age thirty and then again at age fifty and then sixty. Although my mother cautioned me against change, I have gone through change, as will you. That is why it is essential that at some point you should decide on what I call the "givens." These are the beliefs that you hold most dearly at your core. In a different chapter, I am going to give you some advice about relationships, guys, dating, and marriage. Within that realm, these would be the qualities you require most in a guy. On the other hand, they would also be the deal breakers if they don't have them. Before you enter a relationship and think about getting close to a guy even if he makes your heart go pitter-pat, you better have a good idea of what your deal breakers are.

Statistically, I think that change is the primary reason why young marriages are unsuccessful. Young adults fall in love, and that love clouds their judgment about the other person, and even if they see some potential red flags about them, they either overlook them, or they believe they have the power to change them. Big mistake! It is so important that you have a good working relationship with someone you trust, and you can go to them to seek their advice about someone you might be falling in love with. Tell them that your grandfather sent you!

Every day of your life you will make decisions. Some will be very small such as what you are going to wear that day or what flavor of ice cream you order when you're with your boyfriend, Elmer. Other decisions will be major such as choosing a best friend or a college to attend. As you change and grow older, you will look at things differently, and because of that, your decisions will change. Sometimes today I look at decisions I made long ago and wonder why. When your Grandma Becky and I decided to leave Wisconsin and move to western Nebraska, I thought it was a grand adventure as I had just gotten my master's degree in which I wrote a long thesis on Old West American history. When they offered me the job of US History teacher and junior varsity basketball coach, I jumped at it even though many of my friends and colleagues in Wisconsin wondered what the allure was. While at times it was scary, we never regretted the decision. Although we only lived in Alliance for five years, we met some wonderful people there, and both of our lives and careers were broadened greatly. While we were there though, I remember thinking we would never move back, so I withdrew all my Wisconsin retirement account money to buy a new car. Plus, I was only thirty. Who thought much about retirement at that point in their lives anyway? And, it was a brand new Chevy Camaro. I have changed. I look at that decision today as one of the dumbest things I have ever done. (It was a great car!)

Now I am older. My three kids, including your mom, are all grown, and I feel proud of the adults they have all become. They all have graduated from college and are making their way in the professional world. When I look back, I feel like their growing up years went by in about ten minutes. I also feel like I finally get it. And now that I finally get it, nobody cares! That way of thinking is probably what spurred me to leave this book as a legacy to my grandchildren.

One last thing about change. When I was a young teacher, I liked to talk to older staff members. I never wanted to act like I knew everything. I wanted to talk to them about teaching and coaching, and I learned so much from them. They were my mentors, and I am thankful for all their sage advice. A few of the older teachers, those on the verge of retirement, seemed very cynical. Some were upset when they talked about school or teaching. I remember thinking that I never wanted to be that way. I always wanted to be inspired in my teaching of young students, and even though I am now sixty, I think I still am.

CHAPTER 14:
Being Happy

"An optimist is a person who sees a green light everywhere, while the pessimist sees only the red stoplight… the truly wise person is colorblind."

– Albert Schweitzer

Dear Lydia:

There are many things parents and grandparents wish upon their children; financial security; success; and perhaps even breaking a negative cycle of abuse, poverty, or alcoholism. Some parents attempt to relive their own lives through their children. If there is one thing that all parents desire for their children as they watch them leave childhood and enter young adulthood, it is for their children to find true happiness in their lives.

There are a variety of ways to discover happiness. As I watched you recently at your first birthday, two things made you most happy. It wasn't the many gifts that you received. The first was simply the box that one gift came in. You didn't care what was in it. You simply enjoyed climbing onto the box, sliding off, and landing on your diaper-padded butt. You did it over and over again. You were happy. The second thing that gave you obvious pleasure was eating an entire birthday cake by yourself with your hands. Again, you were happy. As your grandfather, nothing makes me happier than to see you excited and happy. One of my own happiest moments was when you started smiling at me and then reaching for me whenever you would see me. If I was ever having a bad day, you cured it instantly.

Give some thought as you grow older to what your needs really are, especially your emotional needs. These needs, which are just as strong as your physical needs, have a major impact on your happiness. If you are in a gloomy or bad mood, it might be that one of your emotional needs is not being met. Give special thought to the difference between your wants and your needs. You may be able to survive without your wants (although your Aunt Alli might dispute this regarding her need to go clothes shopping), but getting by in the long-term without your needs being met is much more difficult.

It seems like some people are never happy. They go out of their way to look for a reason to be unhappy, find the negative in any situation and complain constantly. If you know someone like that, just a heads-up, you won't be able to fix them although you may want to try. I have seen people with emotional barriers. They can often be much greater than mental or physical barriers, and they cause such a burden to the people forced to carry them. Often these people have been scarred by someone or something in their past and cannot work through whatever it is causing them pain. I have known people who have dealt with emotional barriers throughout their entire lives. It is sad to see, but I believe that with time all barriers can be overcome.

Lydia, as I said earlier, all parents want to see their children happy. At the same time, parents can have strong feelings when their child experiences unhappiness or failure. (As a basketball coach I witnessed many parents livid over a perceived injustice to their child.) In my opinion, the most difficult part of parenting is providing the things to your children that you did not have (but wanted) without spoiling them. (As I told you, I grew up shooting hoops, six hundred shots a day, on a dirt court with a hoop nailed to the garage. When your Uncle Wes was old enough and wanted to learn to play basketball, we built a nearly full-sized half court in our backyard complete with a three-point line.)

On one last related note, It is also difficult sometimes to allow your child to experience failure. In fact, that failure can be harder on the parents than it is on the child. Your mom is a lot like me. We think alike, and we both love to compete and win. During Ann's last year in college at UW-Platteville, she was once as high as a seven-time Division III All-American in Track and Field, finishing second once in the 800-meter race in the national meet. She qualified to run in the national meet in Los Angeles, California, and Grandma Becky, your dad, and I went to watch her last collegiate meet. Ann was a great middle-distance runner and university record holder, but for some reason, on that day she didn't run well at all, and she struggled in the race. Afterward, I knew she would not want to see us so we gave her some space, and it took her some time before we found her and were able to talk to her and decompress. We told your mom, who was feeling the harsh sting of defeat, that it was okay. We were just so proud of her and loved her no matter what. Nothing could change that.

CHAPTER 15:
Sports

"Every time you stay out late; every time you sleep in; every time you miss a workout; every time you don't give 100%... you make it that much easier for me to beat you."

– Sign on many locker room walls

Dear Lydia:

You come from a family of sports fanatics. Your Great-Grandfather Papa D Alleman built his own baseball field and has been a lifelong Chicago Cubs fan. Your Great-Grandfather Bill Tank never missed watching his beloved Green Bay Packers and boxed for a time during the 1930s in Sheboygan. Your Grandfather Scott Alleman has played and coached a variety of sports throughout his entire life. I coached basketball for thirty years and am an avid fan of the Wisconsin Badgers, Green Bay Packers, and Milwaukee Brewers. Your mom and dad were both prominent high school and college athletes with your mom achieving Division III All-American status eight times in track. Your Aunt Alli was the captain of the cross country team in college. Your Uncle Wes scored 852 points during his three years of high school varsity basketball. Your second cousin Travis Tank, my brother Mike's son, was drafted by the Milwaukee Brewers after pitching for UW-Whitewater. As you have already observed in your young life, you come from a family known for yelling at the TV during hotly contested games. (I have been known to get up and anxiously leave the room late in games when the Wisconsin Badger basketball teams made their phenomenal runs in back to back Final Fours.) So Lydia, although you may not know yet what all the fuss is about, you come from a family in which sports is important.

Before you were even born, you were in the gym. A few years after retiring as a varsity boys head coach, your mom asked me to come back and help her coach the seventh grade girls team while she was pregnant with you. During the second year of doing that, you were a young eight-month-old who loved coming to practice and the games. You didn't just watch; you were intensely trying to figure out what was going on. Occasionally, when your mom and I would sit the team down to talk to them about the game, you would sit on the side and listen. Every now and then you would join in with an attempt at a word or two. You were never a problem, though. You seemed to enjoy being in the gym, and of course, all the girls on the team thought you were the cutest baby.

Coaches and parents must understand that they are role models for the players on their teams. As a player, I played for two coaches who were both yellers. Their yelling made it difficult to play well because I was often afraid to make a mistake or miss a shot. I thought if I ever got the chance to coach, I wouldn't want to be like that. Then as I became a coach, many people commented that I seemed so calm during games. There were times, however, when I am sorry to say that I lost my cool. At the time, I would say that those moments were premeditated. It was really an act used to fire up my players or intimidate an official. Now I think back to what I did and think, "Man, that was pretty dumb of me." Once during an intense contest, an official's call didn't go our way, so I took my suit coat off (I nearly always wore a suit when I coached) and chucked it to the top of the bleachers. Also, once when an official made a bad call against our team, I called a timeout and didn't even talk to my players. I simply stood there and stared him down across the floor. Unlike me, he handled the situation very well. At the end of the timeout, he came over to me and quietly said that if I ever did that again, he would eject me from the game. All I said was, "Okay," and I never did it again. I feel foolish when I think back to those moments (remember, people change, right?). If you really want to see people acting foolishly, watch a game in which you don't care who wins or loses; you're not emotionally involved. You will see the game entirely differently.

Several pieces of advice to you regarding sports: You won't realize or understand this at first, but while winning or losing is important in sports (I know, why do they keep score and give out trophies?), the most important part of sports is the journey or the process you are going through. Your mom and Aunt Alli were the top two runners on two state championship cross country teams for Dodgeville/Mineral Point. Certainly, it was an awesome experience, and I was a very proud dad as I watched them match each other stride for stride and cross the finish line, but I think it was the many miles of training together that solidly bonded them.

The second piece of sports advice, Lydia, is that I think the best thing someone can say about you is that you were the best teammate on the team. Be that best teammate. During my third year in Alliance, Nebraska, as the head varsity basketball coach, we had a very talented team. There were three starting guards who could shoot the basketball and averaged 27, 20, and 16 points per game. In western Nebraska, not necessarily a high school basketball hotbed, we were a juggernaut that set a state scoring record of about 95 points per game on average. However, I had a player on that team who was not a starter, but without any prompting from me, did everything in his power to encourage his teammates in any way he could. He was vital to the team, and I will always be grateful to him for that.

The third piece of advice is run away from the glitz and glitter as well as other types of showboating which seem so common in sports today. I guess I'm old school, but I just don't like the forty-five minute Super Bowl halftime show or the rock concert given before the NCAA National Championship Basketball Game. To me, it's about the game. It's about work ethic and overcoming obstacles to achieve success. As a coach, I think I always enjoyed teaching the game the most. You know that your mom and dad were and still are excellent runners. Remember that being good at running does not just happen. It's about how much pain you're willing to endure.

Never allow defeat to break you. No one enjoys losing. I have seen athletes' spirits crushed by defeat. The best thing to do when you lose is to resolve to make yourself work harder. I have seen athletes who seem to be lazy, but they are not. They talk a good game about how committed they are, but instead, they hold their emotions back. So much about sports is about your preparation. They don't quite give enough of themselves so that when they aren't successful, and everyone else is in tears, it doesn't hurt so badly.

You may be tempted, and perhaps you will even be invited to play on an elite level team in some sport. The fact that they are pursuing you to play for them or with them can make you feel good about yourself. My advice to you, however, is don't do it. Even though club teams in youth sports and even elite teams have exploded in recent years, I think many of them are a racket. They lure you and your parents in by making you think they are your ticket to a Division I scholarship and a professional career. The odds of you becoming a professional or even getting a college scholarship through athletics are minimal. If that is your dream, go for it, but be wary.

Joe Hanson, who along with Denny McGraw, was your mom's cross country and track coach and an accomplished runner himself, had some excellent insight into your mom's running career and had several points to make regarding your mom's outstanding high school athletic career. "It was obvious early on that Ann was going to be a very good athlete. Denny and I were fortunate that she picked cross country and track. She could have been very good at soccer, softball, or anything she chose, and she was an all-conference basketball player." Very quickly Coach Hanson picked up on other things that took your mother to a higher level. "Ann chose one of the toughest sports there is to excel in. Running is used as a punishment in most sports. She was not one to take the easy way out." Ann had the support of her sister, your Aunt Alli, also a strong cross country runner. Coach Hanson continued, "Ann was a problem solver. To be good at cross country in the fall, you have to work your tail off in the summer." Ann helped Alli, and Alli helped Ann. Together, they figured it out. They were a great example of the whole being greater than the sum of its parts. According to Coach Hanson, "Some people do it without having to be told."

Much like your mom's relationship with your Aunt Alli, your dad was two and a half years younger than your Uncle Doug. They too, while having very different personalities, grew to become very close.

According to your dad, "I used to get so mad at Doug because he was better at things. It was a competition. Doug was always bigger. In pick-up basketball games, fouls were never called on each other. I would never call a foul. We became fierce competitors, and sometimes we would fight. We always seemed to fight and then quickly make up when it was over." As they got older and more mature, your dad and Uncle Doug became even closer. "Doug had a big influence on me. We just seemed to get each other."

Lydia, sports seem so important. I would be surprised if they were not a big part of your life, but it is important to know that if they're not, that's okay too. You are who you are. Your parents and your grandparents will always love you no matter if you score more points in a basketball game or not or if you win races or not. Never forget that. We will be proud of you no matter what!

CHAPTER 16:

Fears

> *"I've failed over and over and over again in my life and that is why I succeed."*
>
> – Michael Jordan

Dear Lydia:

Everyone fears something. It's okay to be afraid. Anyone who acts like they have no fear of anything is either lying or trying to mask their fears. Now, their fears might be different than what you fear, but everyone fears something. Some people think that showing fear makes them look weak. No one wants to be thought of as a coward. As you know, my mother and father raised four sons. I recall my dad saying to us when confronted with something, "Are you afraid?" I look back at that now and think that yes, I probably was, but it was never okay to admit fear. Lydia, my advice to you in this chapter is to admit and confront your fears. Talk to someone about the things you're afraid of. Don't allow your fears to define you. Instead, try to understand why you fear something and then don't run away from it.

So, what are people most often afraid of? Public speaking is a common fear. Some people are terrified to stand up in front of others and speak and will, therefore, avoid it at all costs. When I was in college, I was required to take a speech class. As you recall, I was driven to get As in all of my classes. After giving my first speech, I received a B+, which might have been generous on his part. After talking to the professor, he said that I relied on my notes too much, and the best way to overcome that was to simply have fewer notes in front of me. So, for my second speech I took fewer notes. The problem was I forgot what I was going to say in the middle of my speech. I panicked! I was suddenly filled with fear and mumbled a few things before sitting down. For a long time after that, I feared public speaking. Today, while I don't enjoy it, I find that I am pretty good at it and have given speeches and book talks to various groups.

A second common fear is the fear of failure. Athletes of all ages and abilities face this and can be defeated by it. When you watch a basketball game that is coming down to the final seconds with the score tied or very close, who wants to take the game-winning shot? Quite often, it's not the best or most athletic player on the team. Or you will hear an announcer say that the player who was fouled and is shooting free throws is a 90 percent free throw shooter. That 90 percent shooter only makes one out of two. Fear may have gotten to him or her.

Some players have the innate ability to play without fear and seemingly always come up big at crucial times of games. As a basketball coach, I knew who those players were. On one of the best basketball teams I ever coached, we survived to play in the WIAA State Tournament. Sectional games in which the winner advances to state can be lethal battles. My team had all the pieces we needed to win, but I knew that victory was not guaranteed. In the Sectional Final, Dodgeville played Monona Grove, a much larger school in our division, at Sun Prairie. The game was in one of the loudest high school gyms I had ever been in with fans from both sides yelling well before the game even started. As my players went through the layup and three-point shooting warmup line, fans from Monona Grove taunted my players and especially one who seemed to miss his threes on purpose. They would laugh every time he shot and missed the rim by a foot or more. When the game started, however, this player, who was not the most talented player on the team, but was still very good, was all business. He made three consecutive threes, and the gym rocked with noise from the Dodgeville fans. (Over the years, I have heard some incredibly loud gyms, but on this night this one was the loudest.) We went on to win the game and return to the state tournament. For years now, that player is referred to as the "Assassin" because of his ability to play without fear.

Lydia, your Aunt Alli and your mom led Dodgeville/Mineral Point to two WIAA State Cross Country Championship seasons. They were tireless workers who persevered through grueling workouts to become the best. On the morning of the state meet in Wisconsin Rapids, they were understandably nervous. What if they didn't run well? What if they got out too fast or too slow? They had paced each other throughout their careers, but what if they lost each other during this overcrowded race? They were all about the team's success, and dropping back a place or two could mean the difference between the team finishing second instead of first. They were confident that Dodgeville/Mineral Point was good, but they also had great respect for teams from Tomahawk, Pewaukee, and Shorewood who were just as good. Hours before the race, just after getting their hair braided, and eating pancakes (now I understand where you get your love of pancakes!), I took my two daughters aside and talked to them together. I knew they were nervous, but I did not want them to be afraid. The point of my talk was to reassure them that no matter what happened, win or lose, their mom and I would love them anyway. We were their foundation, which they could count on no matter what.

There are other fears that can prove to be very powerful. Your Great-Grandmother Mary Jane (Doheny) Thompson, a very strong woman, gave her strong fear of cats to Grandma Becky who passed on that fear to your Aunt Alli and your mom. Of course, cats always seem to sense that fear in people and zero in on them when in their presence. Your Aunt Alli turned down lucrative babysitting jobs as a teenager or chose not to go to a friend's party because of the presence of cats.

Conversely, everyone I can think of in my family has a strong fear of mice. Just the thought of a mouse in our house brings fear to Grandma Becky. One April Fool's Day when your mom was in high school, Grandma Becky told your mom, Aunt Alli and me, who were all just getting up and ready for school, that school had been canceled because of excessive flooding in rural areas. At first, I didn't believe her, but she was adamant that it was true. After about five minutes, I started to believe her when she proclaimed, "April fool!" Your mom, Aunt Alli, and I were so mad. You never make jokes about snow days, so we vowed revenge. Over the course of the following year, I purchased a small, fake, but realistic gray mouse. On the night before the next April Fool's Day, I placed that mouse on the toilet seat in the bathroom your Grandma Becky and I use. The next morning, I heard her alarm go off. She got out of bed and walked into the bathroom as I watched with an eye half open. Suddenly she bolted out of the bathroom. She couldn't talk but instead just pointed to the bathroom. I just laughed and laughed. When she realized the joke, she wasn't very happy with me.

I have a mild fear of driving across high or long bridges. I do it, but I'm not comfortable doing it. Once while driving home to Wisconsin from Gulf Shores, Alabama, I accidentally took a wrong turn on the interstate near New Orleans, Louisiana, and ended up driving across the twenty-four mile long Lake Pontchartrain Bridge. I think my knuckles were white the entire time.

So, Lydia, my advice to you is don't allow the fears you may have overcome you; everyone has fears.

CHAPTER 17:
Education

*"Live as if you were to die tomorrow.
Learn as if you were to live forever."*

– Mohandas Gandhi

Dear Lydia:

You are my first grandchild, which is a special relationship, and I love everything about you. As I have gotten to know you during your first year of life, what I enjoy most is simply watching you learn. You are like a sponge soaking in everything. The expression on your face is precious as you point at a bird that flies by or get excited at a person walking their dog. Education is a lifelong process, and you have only just begun your journey. Never be satisfied. Never stop learning. Never think that you have learned enough.

Great-Grandparents Bill and Lydia Tank were both products of the Great Depression. Like many people of that era, they were under severe economic handicaps. For some people, school and education were often seen as "survival of the fittest" with only the strongest surviving academically. In the blue-collar village of Kohler, Wisconsin the children of German immigrants were often looked down upon.

My mother told me a story in which one of her teachers in Kohler, when asked to explain a math problem to her, told my mom that she wasn't very smart in math. Soon my mom believed that. Eighty-five years later, I believe that Lydia Tank was extremely bright and had insights on a variety of different topics, but because she was told by someone whom she either feared or respected that she wasn't smart, she believed it.

After serving in London, England, during the Second World War, Bill Tank returned to Sheboygan, Wisconsin, where he worked for several decades as a foreman in the Pottery Division of the Kohler Company. It was physically exhausting work. He would come home from work, take a shower, and lay down until it was time for dinner (most often large amounts of fried meat and potatoes). It didn't take much for me to figure out and understand that I did not want to do that for the rest of my life. My dad knew that, and one of his best pieces of advice to me regarding education was, "Whatever you have in your head, no one can take away from you." Another was, "Whatever you don't have in your head, you better have in your back and legs." Sometimes I think that students today don't care enough about their education, but would care more and would have a greater appreciation of what school has to offer if they could have met my parents or other people who worked incredibly hard to survive the Great Depression and thrive during the following decades.

While getting an education goes beyond what you learn in school, the value of school in your education is significant. Schooling and degrees are what open doors for you. Competition for jobs is fierce in today's world. Don't limit yourself. You may even be smarter than the person you're competing with for a position, but if you don't have the proper degree, you may not be considered for that position. Sometimes it's difficult to see the need for more schooling, especially when it's so expensive. My advice to you is to get your master's degree or another advanced degree early on after you finish your bachelor's degree. You won't regret it. Your education is most likely the best financial investment you can make.

Never allow anyone to tell you that you are not smart enough, or even worse, let someone tell you that you cannot do something because you're a girl. As I stated earlier, your ability to focus in school is important in determining your success in school. Along the same lines, what is success in school? Without a doubt, grades are very important. You need to show achievement in a rigorous schedule of courses. Challenge yourself and set the bar high. You cannot get to the next level of your education without the grades. Good grades in school should demonstrate that you have learned something. However, there is a subtle difference here. I believe that for all but the very best students, studying is becoming a lost art. It's difficult to study. You need quiet time in a quiet space. To learn, you need to put away the electronic devices. Never study with your cell phone in the same room with the ever-present ding telling you that you just got a text from your boyfriend, Elmer!

I see a growing trend in education where people are putting less and less importance on knowledge. They don't see the need to know something. Their response is often, "Why do I have to know anything about Abraham Lincoln and the Civil War? If I want to know, I can just look it up on my phone." Lydia, resist that attitude and never allow anyone to tell you that knowledge is not important. Most likely the people who are saying that are not as smart as they want you to think they are, and they don't like it when others are smarter than they are.

Dr. Watson Parker, History Professor and my mentor at the UW-Oshkosh, was an incredible teacher who inspired me to learn and go on to teach history. He opened windows for me. As I look back on my relatively brief relationship with the late Dr. Parker, also a noted author and Old West historian, I see a man who always made time to answer my questions. I think he recognized that I was at a turning point in my life, and I can recall leaving one-on-one meetings with him at his office and feeling in awe of this man. I was so inspired. I was transitioning from recent high school graduate to becoming a historian in my own right. I worked for him using federal government work-study money for three years (something for which I will always be grateful) during which I wrote a nearly 150-page index to *Bits and Pieces*, a Black Hills history magazine. After gaining eighteen graduate credits in history at Marquette University, I returned to UW-Oshkosh to complete my master's degree under the supervision of Dr. Parker while I was teaching in Plymouth. One of my regrets is that I did not give more back to him. He impacted my life that much.

The best educators must have excellent communication skills.

The most underrated but most necessary skill of a good communicator is the ability to listen. Dr. Parker and other excellent educators with whom I have had the honor to work with over the years have all been good listeners. As we go deeper now into the twenty-first century, never forget the importance of the ability to communicate and listen, skills which are depreciating as people spend more and more time on their phones and other devices. On a related note, in an upcoming chapter, I'm going to give you some advice about guys and dating. I will say it right now, though. I don't care how good-looking he is or is not, run away (if you take after your mom and dad, you will be a fast runner!) from the guy who doesn't listen to you and constantly talks about himself. Most people talk way more than they listen.

There are many ways in which you can learn. If you find a learning style that works for you, that's great. Just don't be afraid to branch out and expand your horizons now and then. Most importantly, always ask questions. Questions are food for your brain. A few other students may get annoyed with you for being the one who always asks questions. They may even give you the "eye roll" for asking another question. Ignore them. My bet, however, is that there was more than one student who had the same question but was afraid to speak up.

Lydia, as you begin to understand the world of learning, you will be exposed to many new things. Remember your Great-Grandmother Lydia Tank's words of wisdom, "Always remember who you are and where you came from." I think the greatest mistake many people make is that they think they are smarter and simply know more than everyone else. While Dr. Parker was a nationally known historian, I remember how he was never stuck on himself. I never felt like he thought that he was above anyone else. When I introduced him to my parents as one of the great influences in my life when I was graduating from college, he was very cordial, kind, and gracious, and I miss him.

Someone told me once that it doesn't matter how much you know if you don't pass it on. I like that. Perhaps those words influenced me to write this book to you.

CHAPTER 18:
Reading

*"My alma mater was books, a good library…
I could spend the rest of my life reading,
just satisfying my curiosity."*

– Malcolm X

Dear Lydia:

I tell my high school students that quite often the highlight of my week is driving forty-five minutes to the Barnes and Noble bookstore in Madison on Saturday morning where I buy a grande vanilla latte and look at books before deciding which ones to buy and read. When I told that to one class of sixteen- and seventeen-year-olds, a girl from a highly educated family, who would go on to UW-Madison, looked at me with this incredulous look and simply stated, "Why?" I was slightly stunned. Here was someone who was planning to attend a Big Ten university and had no concept of how someone could get pleasure or inspiration from expanding their mind through reading. She just didn't get it.

Within Barnes and Noble there are various sections for everyone's tastes in reading. Being a history teacher, I always have a pretty good idea of what is currently available in the history, current issues, sociology, education, and biography sections. Lately, I have discovered a great interest in reading memoirs written by people with an interesting story to tell. There is one section there, however, that makes me cringe whenever I read the sign. It says, "Books That Make You Think." I guess my thought is, aren't all books supposed to make you think? Why would I read a book if it didn't make me think? Even better, the best books will help you gain a greater understanding of yourself and other people around you. To answer the girl I mentioned earlier, that is why I enjoy reading!

Lydia, my advice to you is to read, and read a lot. Thirty-five years ago, in 1982, early in my teaching career and while I was working on my master's degree, I bought a spiral notebook and started keeping track of the books I read. At the time, I had no idea that I would do this for the rest of my life and was creating a historical artifact for future generations to peruse. Early on while doing this, I set a goal for myself (remember how goal oriented I am!) to read fifty books a year. While fifty sounded daunting, I broke it down to about four books a month or a book a week. Throughout the past thirty-five years, there have only been a few times when I failed to reach that goal. Most often I exceeded fifty, and I am not far from filling my second notebook. Occasionally, I will go back and look at what I read years ago. Sometimes I can't even remember what a specific book was about. Other times I'm reminded of a certain book which I had enjoyed. Most often I notice changes in my reading patterns. I read certain types of books twenty years ago, but they have been replaced by a different type of book today. To you, I would say it doesn't matter what type of book you read. Just read, and read a lot.

Try to make reading a priority. When the topic of reading comes up, one common reaction I hear from people is that they admire the fact that I read that much and want to themselves, but they just don't have time to read. The funny part is that those people are often the ones I see checking their social media sites or wasting time in other ways. I always try to read at least twenty pages before going to school in the morning. You could wake up thirty minutes earlier each morning to read. Or if you're more of a night person, you could stay up thirty minutes longer. Again, what can you do to make reading a priority?

It's easy to get bogged down if a book is not very interesting or if the number of pages is too daunting, but please understand that not every book I read is a great book. (For me, if a book is more than three hundred pages, I force myself to get through the first hundred pages as quickly as possible. Once I do that, I'm usually drawn into the book.) I categorize the books I read into three groups. The first group includes books that are perhaps just okay but wouldn't recommend to others. Unfortunately, I have read a number of those books. If I'm reading fiction, which I do on occasion, and there are simply too many characters to follow, I get lost and cannot keep them straight.

My second group consists of very good books and books from which I may have learned a lot. If it's a history book, I probably underlined a lot of information or used it for my history class lectures. When I'm about to teach an upcoming history unit, I try to read a book or two about some topic in that unit beforehand. For instance, Joseph Ellis has written *Founding Brothers* among other excellent books on the Revolutionary War period of American history, and I will often pick up one of them before teaching that time period.

The third group of books I read is made up of the best of the best. These are books that inspire me. They are the ones that I cannot put down while I'm reading them. Often, I will say to myself, "Oh my gosh!" and then two or three pages later I say, "Oh my gosh!" again. These books change the way I think about things, and not only give great insight into a topic but might inspire me to make a difference in other people's lives. For instance, *Just Mercy* by Bryan Stevenson was a book which made me question the injustice of capital punishment and corruption in the American court system. Another book, *Evicted: Poverty and Profit in an American City* by Matthew Desmond, did such a great job of showing what homeless people and the working poor in Milwaukee suffer through. Reading it made me want to go to Milwaukee and do whatever I could to help people who were less fortunate than I am. Read the books in this group more than once.

You will know what you like. You will know that what is best for me might not be good for you. On the other hand, what you like and is meaningful to you right now might not be so in a year or two. (I still have the Chip Hilton sports series in which I, in seventh grade, wrote in one of the basketball books, "This is the best book I have ever read!") Also, don't be afraid to branch out and read something that is out of your area of interest. You might surprise yourself and like something new. I like to ask other people what the best book that they have ever read is. (I am always surprised when eighteen-year-old high school seniors who are going on to college tell me that they have never read an entire book.) On the plus side, Dodgeville High School students know that I read, and many have come to me for recommendations if they are looking for something good. Yes, I lend them my books, and I have lost more than a few by doing so, but if I ask them later if they liked a particular book I recommended and their eyes light up, to me it's all worth it.

Lydia, English teachers probably won't like to hear this, but I don't like reading the classics. If you can establish a goal of reading the classics as some people do, good for you. With a few exceptions (one being Margaret Mitchell's *Gone With the Wind*, a 1,000-page novel of the Civil War Era given to me by Grandma Lydia), they're just not for me. My advice to you is to make your own classics. Again, read and read a lot.

Over the past thirty-five years I have read nearly two thousand books. Which books or authors are the best and recommended to you?

- *Half the Sky: Turning Oppression into Opportunity for Women Worldwide* by Nicholas Kristof and Sheryl WuDunn. Lydia, this book does a great job explaining how different your life as a girl in Dodgeville, Wisconsin, is in comparison to other areas of the world.

- *Generation Me: Why Today's Young Americans are More Confident, Assertive, Entitled – and More Miserable Than Ever Before* by Jean M. Twenge, Ph.D. Lydia, so many people of older generations wonder what is wrong with today's generation of kids. This book does a great job of explaining that.

- *Confessions of an Economic Hit Man* by John Perkins. Because of the constant terrorist threat, we live in an age of fear. This book gives numerous reasons why people from other cultures strongly dislike the United States.

- *Glow Kids: How Screen Addiction is Hijacking Our Kids – And How to Break the Trance* by Nicholas Kardaras, Ph.D. Every parent should read this book before buying their child an iPhone.

- *Newtown: An American Tragedy* by Matthew Lysiak. School shootings in which innocent people are terrorized and sometimes killed are awful. They are every parent and teacher's nightmare. This book chronicles the 2012 crime spree at Sandy Hook Elementary School in Newtown, Connecticut.

- *His Needs, Her Needs* by Willard F. Harley, Jr. Choosing the person with whom you will spend the rest of your life is a decision most people make at some point in their lives. Of the many books on relationships I have read, I recommend reading this book before getting married.

- *The Glory and the Dream* by William Manchester. This history book vividly chronicles American history from the Stock Market Crash in 1929 to the Watergate scandal of 1972. William Manchester was one of my favorite authors and one of a few writers from whom I read everything they wrote simply because they wrote it.

- *A Stillness at Appomattox* by Bruce Catton. Anything on the Civil War by Bruce Catton is very good. His words stoked a fire in me to learn history many years ago.

- *The Worst Hard Time: The Untold Story of Those Who Survived the Great American Dust Bowl* by Timothy Egan. Most people have no idea just how critical the 1930s was and what people had to endure.

- *A Season on the Brink: A Year with Bob Knight and the Indiana Hoosiers* by John Feinstein. Lydia, if you ever consider becoming a college athlete, read this book. Feinstein has written a number of excellent sports books, but this one is my all-time favorite.

- *The Pilot's Wife* by Anita Shreve. I don't read a lot of fiction, but if I see anything new come out by Anita Shreve, I buy it automatically. Her stories are not difficult to follow, and she gives great insight into how people think.

- *Lies at the Altar: The Truth about Great Marriages* by Robin Smith. When you decide to marry someone, your vision will be clouded. You will probably be very happy. This book should be read before you say, "I do."

Again, these are the books that are the best for me. Ten years ago I might have given you a totally different list of best books and ten years from now another list. Know what books are best for you. My advice to you is to keep a notebook with the titles of the books you read. There are many ways to learn, but if you don't read, you are limiting yourself. Lastly, I urge you to read about people who worked to overcome difficulty. Seeing that there are people in the world who have faced adversity far greater than you or I can ever imagine helps you to appreciate your own life.

CHAPTER 19:
Religion

*"Without faith a man can do nothing;
with it all things are possible."*

– Sir William Osler

Dear Lydia:

This is not an easy chapter to write because everyone has their own personal belief system and is entitled to those beliefs. Those beliefs may evolve throughout your life. They may change as you get older or as events shape your life. Who am I to say that mine are right and yours are wrong? That is not my intention at all. What I would like you to consider is what my faith in God is and how that impacts my daily life.

Your Great-Grandma Lydia Tank had the strongest faith in God of anyone I ever knew. She sang in the church choir, taught Sunday school, and was a regular attending member at St. Paul's Evangelical Lutheran Church in Sheboygan Falls, Wisconsin, until her death and funeral there in 1980. She also "walked the talk." She raised her four boys by taking us to Sunday school, which she taught, and church services there. Swearing was something we were never allowed to do, and if we did and she heard us, there would be trouble. One time when I was in about fifth grade, I was involved with some neighbor boys in a heated basketball game out in our driveway. It was a warm afternoon, and my mom was in the kitchen cooking one of her delicious dinners with the windows open. We were playing a game of two-on-two in which the first team to score ten points won. Well, the game got more and more heated. Sweat poured off the four eleven-year-old boys. With the score tied at nine all, I got the ball not far from the hoop. I faked my defender, took one dribble and shot a fairly easy and makeable potentially game-winning shot. I thought I had made it, but instead, the ball clanked off the rim. I couldn't believe it and yelled, "Oh, shit!" Although it happened nearly fifty years ago, I remember it like it happened yesterday. My mother stormed out of the house and onto the driveway court. She quickly told the boys they had to leave, and as my jaw dropped, she grabbed me by the ear and hauled me into the kitchen (I'm not sure my feet were touching the ground as she did so) to sit on a chair until dinner time. When I feebly tried to explain to her that it was game point, she didn't want to hear it. For the rest of my life, lesson learned.

On a related note, as your mom and Aunt Alli were reaching their early elementary school years, they too came to hear certain bad words from other kids on the school playground. Wanting to raise them with the same values we had learned growing up, we told them that there were certain words they were never allowed to say. Their ears perked up, and a short time later your mom came running up to me with what seemed to be really big news. "Dad! Dad!" she yelled. "Alli said the f-word!" I looked at her with questioning concern on my face and said, "What? She didn't." Your mom said, "Yes, she did! She said, 'fart.'" I couldn't help but laugh.

Throughout the years as a high school basketball coach most would say that I was known for keeping my composure. I always wanted that poise to be reflected by my players on the court. Because of that, I tried my best to never swear in front of my players like many coaches are known to do. It just seemed hypocritical to me if players asked for a moment of silence or prayer before taking the floor in a big game, and then I swore at them during the heat of battle, so I tried very hard not to do it. Especially in some of my more animated halftime speeches, I became well known for my angry "gosh darn its" or "gol dang its." One incident, in particular, stands out. During a game late in our 2005 undefeated regular season at our bitter rival River Valley's gym in Spring Green, we were not playing very well, and I knew Valley would like nothing better than to avenge a loss to us earlier in the season. We were very lethargic, and at halftime we went into the locker room with the score tied. I knew I had to do something to get our team fired up, to arouse their emotions and get them angry. After talking briefly to my assistant coaches who all agreed that we just weren't fired up, I followed the team into the locker room. As I walked in and strode to the front of the room to address the team, there was absolute silence. I had gotten into the habit of bringing a can of Coke along to games and would drink some before the game and then more at the half. Well, I went to the locker where the can was and took a sip as I angrily walked to the front of the room. I was steaming. I don't remember what I said, but I know I took the can of Coke and, being careful not to hit anyone with it, I threw it as hard as I could straight downward. The can was probably three-quarters full, so the soda shot straight upward and got all over the side of my face and ear. So here I was as angry as I could be, wearing a suit and tie, and yelling at the players with Coke dripping off my ear. The players still talk about how they were all doing their best not to laugh and had to look away as I was yelling at them. At least we played better in the second half and won the game.

Lydia, my advice to you is to stay away from people who combine politics and religion. I am a Christian, and I believe that through a miracle I was put here on earth to carry out God's will. Prayer is the best way to find out what that will may be, and it is a good thing to pray regularly to find out what God's will is. I also think that you cannot pray only when you want or need something. I don't think that's how it works.

Through my Christian faith, I have come to believe that God is a loving God. He knows you and me far better than anyone one else can. I also believe that God has a great sense of humor. When your mom was not even a year old, and your Aunt Alli was barely two years old, we had just moved to Dodgeville and joined Grace Lutheran Church. On one Sunday, the five of us packed our crayons and baggies of Cheerios and went to the eight o'clock service and sat in the back. After one seemingly endless Lutheran hymn, we were all sitting back down as the church got quiet, and Grandma Becky accidentally knocked the box of crayons off the pew, sending them scattering on the tile floor. Again, the church had just gotten quiet, and Grandma Becky reacted instinctively by saying, "Oh, shit!" I thought a lightning bolt might come through the ceiling, but later I was glad that God must've had a sense of humor.

While I do not believe that God is going to intervene to help a certain team win a game, I do believe that there is a spirit, call it a guardian angel if you want, who is always present. Whenever I coached, during the playing of the National Anthem, I would always look at the flag and have a silent talk with my spirits. If it was a big game like a sectional final, I would internally talk to my parents and ask them to help my players play as well as they could. I think the first time I did that was the 1995 WIAA Sectional Final against then bitter rival Cuba City at Wisconsin Dells. My cousin Jack Capelle was the coach in the Dells then. Jack's dad, Wally Capelle, had been the longtime chief of police in Kohler, Wisconsin, and had died years earlier. To gain the right to play in the state tournament was a great thing of which all my players had dreamed, but to beat a huge rival coached by Jerry Petitgoue, the winningest coach in state history, was beyond my wildest dreams. After beating them that night in the Dells, I remember thinking that my mom, dad, and Uncle Wally all had something to do with it, and I was most grateful. I am convinced that their spirits were with me that night in March 1995.

I believe that their spirits remain with us after they are gone. As my brother Jim was dying of cancer in 2015, your Grandma Becky and I went to visit him one last time. It was a day in which it would rain for a few minutes, and then the sun would shine brightly. I hadn't seen him in more than a few years and wasn't exactly sure where in Sheboygan he lived. As I drove around on the south side of Sheboygan and was about to see my brother for the last time, I turned a street corner, and suddenly a giant rainbow arched across the sky in front of me. I was sure that the spirits of Lydia and Bill Tank were talking to me. Also, when I sat on your mom and dad's deck, and they told me stories about when your dad was a boy, again suddenly a giant rainbow became visible. We thought it was probably your Great-Grandma Jeanne Alleman, who had passed away not too long ago, speaking to us.

Lydia Jeanne, you were named after two women who both possessed great spirit. I believe that spirit carries on within you. The spirit of the Lord is an awesome thing filled with love. It will always be with you. Listen to it. If I have any choice or say in the matter, when I die I will be the one watching over you.

CHAPTER 20:
Pleasing Your Parents

> *"You never appreciate your parents' good sense and wisdom, until you miss an opportunity where you needed it the most."*
>
> – Cyntoria Brown

Dear Lydia:

You come from a family of pleasers. Pleasers are people who put the needs and desires of others before themselves. They are selfless. If ten people are waiting in line, the pleaser will be last. I think your mom and dad are both pleasers. When I spoke to Dodgeville/Mineral Point Cross Country Coach Joe Hanson about your mom and what made her the great person she is, the first thing he said was, "Ann is a pleaser. She does not want to disappoint anyone." Nearly always when you ask her what she would like to do or where she would like to eat, she automatically replies, "I don't care," allowing the desires of someone else to come first.

Pleasers connect with one another and understand each other. Your Great-Grandmother Lydia Tank and I were both the pleasers in the family. It's why I do not enjoy celebrating my birthday or Father's Day. If I could celebrate Christmas by buying gifts for everyone else without getting any in return, I would do so. Now, while I love each of my three children equally, it's also probably why your mom and I have such a strong connection. You may become a pleaser as well. I don't know yet. That is yet to be seen. As a pleaser, my advice to you is that while it's not a good thing to be selfish, be wary of always putting your needs and wants last.

Pleasers want to make others around them happy, especially children with their parents. They want to know that their achievements are appreciated. It is important, Lydia, that you know that you will always be loved unconditionally. One of the first things I said to you when I held you and talked quietly to you on that spring day in 2016 was, "I am always going to love you." That is a given no matter what your grades in school are or other achievements may be. You will be loved.

Understand that you are extremely fortunate to have been born to two great parents who are also genuinely good people. As you grow up, there will be times when you may not agree with decisions they make regarding you (even your mom, as good as she was, went into her bedroom and slammed the door on occasion), and as everyone does, there will be times when they make mistakes. It is, however, important that you know that you are deeply loved, and they have your best interests in mind. (By the way, when that happens, and hopefully I am still around, feel free to come over to my house and emotionally vent to your grandfather. I'm a good listener!)

Both of your parents are teachers and coaches in a small town. Your grandfather is a Wisconsin Basketball Coaches Hall of Fame coach and longtime high school history teacher. As I said earlier, you were born somewhat of a small-town celebrity baby. This means that as you grow up, people you don't even know will know you. For example, when I was younger, I used to enjoy driving sports cars. Grandma Becky and I owned four Mustangs and three Camaros over the years before I gave them up. Well, when your Uncle Wes turned sixteen and got his driver's license, he asked if he could borrow the Mustang to run a quick errand. I said he could. A short time later I got a call from a friend saying that Wes had done a "California stop" through a stop sign. He got home a few minutes later, and I asked him about his driving and told him about the call. He couldn't believe it. Lydia, the point is that if you do something in a small town, people will know just because of who you are.

Some adults and other kids may also think that you are favored or entitled just because of who you are. Stand up to that way of thinking. Always do what is right. Stand up for the underdog. You choose what is best for you. You make your mark. Use the skills, strengths, and qualities which you possess to accomplish everything you set your mind to achieve. I believe that willpower, determination, and perseverance are the most underrated qualities anyone can possess.

On the other hand, the bar is set high. More will be expected of you just because of who you are, and if you are naturally a pleaser, it may even be more difficult. As I said in my first book, *Coaching Our Sons*, your Uncle Wes thought it was tough playing basketball for his dad. He said that if he was shooting well and had a good game, it was generally overlooked by people because he was expected to do that as the coach's son. If he didn't shoot as well and struggled in the game, he thought people were saying that the only reason he was on the court was because he was the coach's kid. He felt that the deck was stacked against him. Other coaches I interviewed said similar things about their sons.

CHAPTER 21:
Toughness

"Sports do not build character. They reveal it."

– John Wooden

Dear Lydia:

As you grow up, you will hear a lot about being tough. No one likes to be thought of as weak. As an athlete, one of the worst things you can say about a person in any sport is that they're not tough. As a coach, I have heard and seen players say they are fine and ready to return to action when in fact they are badly hurt. The worst athletic injury I ever saw was when your Grandma Becky was training to run her eighteenth marathon, a 26.2-mile race. During one of her last lengthy training runs, she tripped on a mat covering the high school track. As she fell hard on the track, she dislocated her left elbow and fractured it in two places. It was a compound fracture, which meant that it was bleeding at the point of fracture. Obviously, your grandma was in tremendous pain. Since she could not stand up, it was lucky that two ladies were also walking the track at 6:45 a.m. and were able to call 911 as well as me at the high school. When I got there, one of the first things Grandma Becky said to me was, "Be sure to tell them to put a small cast on my arm so I can still run in the race in a few weeks." Of course, I reassured her that I would do that while thinking that there was no way she would ever be ready for that race. In the end, she did not run the race, and for a time it nearly ended her running career.

Lydia, never make the mistake of thinking that boys are tougher than you simply because they may be bigger, louder, meaner, or have more defined muscles than you do. I will talk more about boys in a later chapter, but as a general rule, a lot of boys are insecure, and the ones who appear to be the toughest or loudest are the most insecure. Ask that meanest and toughest sounding guy to stand up and give a speech in front of a crowd of strangers, and see how tough he is.

I am a big believer that mental toughness is three or four times more important than physical toughness. People who can overcome their fears and other ailments without all the acclaim that goes with it are mentally tough. My guess is that mental toughness was much more common with members of the Greatest Generation, made up of the people who lived through the Great Depression and the Second World War, two of the most difficult and emotionally traumatic events in American history. They never quit. Instead, they battled their way through. They were survivors. Yet, for the most part, they didn't talk about it. They simply did what they had to do and moved on. I like that.

Your Great-Grandmother Lydia Tank was a member of that generation, and she was the most mentally tough person I ever knew. She fought the disease purpura along with the stigma that came with it and the strangers who stared at her because of the red blotches on her face and skin. It wasn't pretty, and she knew it, but she endured it without complaint. She was the third daughter of working-class German immigrants Gottlieb Seidenzahl and Emma Rau, and this was her lot in life until her death at age fifty-nine in 1980, only nine months after your Grandma Becky and I got married.

When I teach my students in my history classes about the 1930s, I talk about the struggles people had to deal with, and I show them images which reflect their utter despair in which they often did not know where to turn or from where their next meal would come. I ask them to reflect on their own lives. What is the greatest crisis they have ever faced? (My answer to them is that their great crisis is losing their cell phone!) No one knows how they will react when they're faced with a crisis.

So how do you build mental toughness? It's a question not easily answered and one worth considering. Some parents physically and emotionally abuse their kids while thinking they are creating toughness. Wrong. All they are doing is creating people who will most likely go on to abuse their children. Others rarely are there as a support for their child when they fall or scrape their knee because they believe they are creating a weak child. Meanwhile, I think it's more common today for parents to want to rescue their child or keep them from feeling any physical or emotional pain. As I have watched you recently learn to walk, I saw you stumble and fall a time or two. Your mom and dad handled it beautifully. If it was a nasty bump, they were there to comfort you. If it wasn't too bad, but you cried a little anyway, your mom was likely to say, "You're fine. Get back up." And you did. To me, I saw a little girl who was expanding her horizons and at the same time had the seeds of toughness planted.

In sports, you often hear about mental toughness. I will take a mentally tough team made up of players who are less talented or smaller over a team with great athletes and more skilled players but are mentally weak anytime. I have been a part of seven state basketball tournaments, having coached in five. There is a saying in sports that goes, "In the big games, big players play big." I interpret that as meaning mentally tough players rise up. Over my thirty years of coaching, the best teams I coached had mentally tough players. On a long bus ride home after a hard-fought victory over a highly ranked opponent in a sectional semifinal basketball game and the night before playing the final, I remember walking to the back of the bus to talk to a few of my most mentally tough players. I asked them, "Well, how strong do your shoulders feel, because tomorrow night we're going to have to climb on them." Later they told me that the hair on the backs of their necks stood up. The following night in the sectional final to go to the State Tournament, we won the game.

Running is one indicator of mental toughness. Sometimes coaches, including myself, try to punish their athletes by making them run more. (When your mom and Aunt Alli were young girls, they would ask me to give them a ride in the car across town the mile or so to the swimming pool on a hot summer day. They would get so angry with me, thinking I was so unfair, because I would tell them, "No, ride your bike. It will put steel in your legs." It did.) When you feel like a coach is punishing you unfairly, my advice to you, Lydia, is to show your coach that running cannot be a punishment by running farther or longer than what was required.

Only mentally tough people can run marathons. A 26.2-mile race is grueling and can break even the toughest runners. Only the best can qualify to run in the best. You come from a family of runners. While I ran two marathons, your Grandma Becky has run seventeen, including the elite Boston Marathon. Your Aunt Alli, Uncle Patrick Klein, and your mom and dad have all run marathons, including Boston, which you attended as an eleven-month-old, and watched in April 2017. They have demonstrated their mental toughness. There is already talk in the family that someday there might be three generations running the Boston Marathon together.

CHAPTER 22:

Work Ethic

"Far and away the best prize that life has to offer is the chance to work hard at work worth doing."

– Theodore Roosevelt

Dear Lydia:

Your work ethic is just about as important as who you are as a person and what others think of you. On the other hand, one of the worst things anyone else can say about you, especially an athlete, is that you are lazy. Many things in life are beyond your control, but how hard you work is one of the most important things within your control. My advice to you is to make your work ethic a priority in your life. Never allow anyone else to work harder than you do to gain or achieve something. Whether it's an A on a test in a difficult Advanced Placement course or a number one runner spot on the cross country team, your work ethic, established early, will carry over into the rest of your life.

At some point while I was growing up in blue-collar Sheboygan Falls during the 1960s, as I watched my dad go to work every day at the Kohler Company, it dawned on me that to get what I wanted in life, I didn't have to be smarter than anyone else or more talented than anyone else. However, I decided that no one was going to work harder than I did. I consciously told myself that if I was going to make my mark in life, I might not have the advantages other kids might have, but I would outwork them. I also felt that if I somehow fell short of my goals, at least I could say that I had done everything possible to achieve them, but things just weren't meant to be. No regrets.

As a history teacher, I have been fortunate enough to have worked with thousands of young people. It is a great joy for me to "watch the light bulb go on" for many students as they learn history in a more in depth manner. Many have told me they have never enjoyed learning history until this class. Especially for my advanced placement students, the amount of history they are required to know to pass the advanced placement exam is staggering, probably more than I knew in my freshman level history courses in college. From day one in the class, I tell the students to avoid shortcuts and never be satisfied that they know enough. As a general rule, study, study, and then study some more. Every year I am pleasantly surprised at the number of students, including many sophomores, who listen to my advice and how well it works out for them.

When I was in high school in Sheboygan Falls in the early 1970s, there were no advanced placement courses offered there, but I was still inwardly driven to get the best possible grades. I wanted "A's". I recall my guidance counselor wincing when I told him that my goal was to become a history teacher because following the end of the Vietnam War in 1973 there was a glut of teachers in the job market. I also recall a school administrator, when I asked him what it would take to get a history teaching job, told me that while many people were looking for jobs, there was always room for the best. So, I set out to become the best, and the first step was to get the best possible grades in school.

By the time I was a senior ready to graduate and move on, I was near the top of my graduating class, although I am pretty sure that I didn't even know that at the time. Now, while I loved social studies and English courses, science courses were not easy for me. That year my most difficult class, taught by an excellent teacher, was Human Anatomy and Physiology. There was a lot of memorization of body parts and their functions which required a lot of work to learn. The exams in the class were published exams by the textbook publisher, which I thought made it even more difficult at the time. A 90% was the standard required in courses to get an "A" in a class. Throughout my four years, I think I was a career 90 percent student. I studied hard to earn the "A" in the class. In March, 1975, Sheboygan Falls was engulfed in basketball fever or "March Madness" when our team qualified for its second consecutive WIAA State Tournament. I was a member of the team, but I was still pretty concerned about an upcoming comprehensive exam in Human Anatomy and Physiology. So as an eighteen-year-old boy who loved basketball, what did I do? I took my books and notebook along to Madison and studied Human Anatomy and Physiology in a lounge area of the Sheraton Inn where we were staying. When I relate that story to my students today, they have a difficult time believing me, but it's true. I was driven, and I had the work ethic.

Lydia, when I went off to college in the fall of 1975 as a history education major, one of the first things I did was to introduce myself to the Chairperson of the History Department and said that my goal was to become a history teacher. He was a very nice man who welcomed me to Oshkosh, but I was surprised that, like my high school guidance counselor, he immediately attempted to talk me out of becoming a history teacher. He said that history is a good liberal arts major and works well for graduates who would perhaps go on to manage a restaurant such as McDonald's. My jaw dropped. No offense to all of the hardworking McDonald's workers out there, but I had no intention of working four years in college and then getting a job in fast food.

I had developed a passion for history, and I wanted to learn everything I could. My strong work ethic kicked in. In college, I still wanted the best grade point average I could get. Even as a freshman in the dorms, I studied as much as I could, and I was not much of a partier. Much like today, on weekends, I would set up a study and workout schedule to maximize my time. I would get up early every day and start studying and reading even as most of my friends slept off their fun times from the night before. In my history classes, I was told to know everything. When the syllabus for one introductory semester class in the history department was handed out, we were told that our grade in the course was to be based on three cumulative exams, one given about every six weeks or so. Anything given in lecture or the corresponding chapters in the textbook was fair game for the tests. Unlike a few of my friends who didn't study nearly as much (I could never understand why for some people not studying is worn as a badge of honor), I would create lists of everything I needed to know and start reviewing weeks in advance. As it happened, I think I got a B on the first test but luckily an "A" on the last two so I aced the course.

That last work ethic example reminds me of an important piece of advice. With anything in life, you will suffer setbacks. Don't expect your mom or dad or anyone to come swooping in to rescue you. Always remember that in sports you learn more from a loss than you do from a victory. As a basketball coach, losses sting, but I did some of my best teaching, and my players worked harder after we lost the previous game.

CHAPTER 23:
Entitlement

> *"Many young people also display entitlement, a facet of narcissism that involves believing that you deserve and are entitled to more than others."*
>
> – Jean M. Twenge, Ph.D. author of *Generation Me*

Dear Lydia:

You were born into a time and a culture which foster a growing gap between the wealthy and the poor, the "haves" and the "have-nots." Historically, this gap has always been there. What I am seeing more so today is that the less fortunate are being demonized by the people economically above them. In other words, it's their fault. If those people would just somehow work harder or had developed a better work ethic, they could better themselves. I could not disagree more. Quite often those people who have "made it" are the children or grandchildren of the generation who had struggled, but they have somehow lost sight of that fact, and they believe that they are somehow better because they are now within a higher economic class. Please do not misunderstand me; not all wealthy people are like this. Perhaps most are not. In my opinion, it's the people who want others to think they have money who act most entitled.

By now you have a pretty good understanding of the side in which I was born and raised, although it was during a time in America when there was much less stigma involved. As Great-Grandmother Lydia Tank offered to me a long time ago as I went off to college and walked through a door of economic opportunity, "Never forget who you are and where you came from." Because of that, I bristle at any hint of entitlement or when I see young people acting like someone owes them something, a pretty common sight in today's world.

Nothing gives me more pleasure than when I can help other people, especially those who are less fortunate than I am. Even if that means something minor such as holding one or both of the double doors at Barnes and Noble open for an elderly or disabled person attempting to manipulate their walker through them. Those people are always very appreciative. However, nothing gets me fired up more quickly than people who act like I owe them something.

As a longtime educator, I get invited along with your Grandma Becky to many graduation parties of graduating seniors every year. To me, it's always an honor to get invited to their party, and, although it's not possible to go to all of them, I try to attend and give a small gift of a card with money to each one. As a teacher, it is always my goal to make a positive difference in the lives of each of my students. By being invited to share in their celebration, I feel like I have accomplished something, and I am especially happy to be invited into the homes of those students who had more difficulty getting through high school. Those are the students who present themselves with the least amount of entitlement.

All parents want their children to be successful in this world, whatever that means. To some, it might mean money. It seems like our American society today focuses on money and the accumulation of more stuff. To others, it might mean happiness. Regardless, I have long believed that the most difficult point of parenting is to provide my kids the material things which I did without as a boy without them becoming spoiled. Although they never said so at the time, today your Uncle Wes, Aunt Alli, and your mom have said on occasion that we may have erred on the side of spoiling them. Yes, we bought them things on our many trips to West Towne Mall, but your Grandma Becky and I always said that we would buy them what we could, but as soon as anyone acted like we owed them something, we were done. None of them ever did.

I believe that a growing trend in recent years is that there are so many athletes who feel entitled. When they try out for a team sport, there is an expectation that they will not only make the team, but they will play and perhaps even become a star. Parents want their child to have the edge over others their own age. Kids are pushed into sports leagues at younger and younger ages. There is a pervasive feeling that if they don't do it, others will, and their child will get left behind. By the time they enter high school, their kids have been playing organized, competitive sports for seven years or more. Parents have spent thousands of dollars on traveling sports teams to help their child be successful in that sport. When the time then comes for that child to play in high school, they may not even enjoy the sport anymore. They may even quit. Who gets blamed? The coach does because the child may have experienced great success as he or she came up the line, but with the high school coach, they did not.

Feeling entitled can become a barrier to success. As I stated in the last chapter, nothing can effectively replace a solid work ethic when it comes to finding success. Nothing. Of course, having a great work ethic does not guarantee success, especially in high school athletics, but having a feeling of entitlement practically guarantees failure. Time and again I have been told by parents who have their own history of athletic achievements that they sent their child to a certain camp, or they're playing on an elite team (elitism is another form of entitlement). Recently I spoke with a mother whose son played on an elite baseball team for sixteen-year-olds and was already getting "looks" from area Division I colleges. The mother said she had spent $28,000 over the previous year to increase her son's chances. I asked her if she ever regretted spending that much, and she replied, "Not at all. If he gets a scholarship, it's money well spent." While I will never know if she was successful in gaining the scholarship for her son, I did feel sorry for the baseball coach who would have to put up with the boy if he struck out over the next two years.

Lydia, my main advice to you here is to never think that you're any better than anyone else. Always treat others with respect and especially in athletics. If you are competing against a team that has less talent than your team, and their win/loss record isn't nearly as good as yours, never believe anyone who tells you, as they will, that you should win easily. That's exactly how you get beaten. I have seen this happen to some pretty talented athletes and some pretty good teams. Why? By thinking they are entitled, they have set themselves up for failure. There are many variables which can influence high school athletic contests. Entitlement and the corresponding arrogance are the first two, and two you can and should eliminate.

Lydia, lastly on this topic, my first note of advice to you regarding dating and boys is that if you ever date a guy who seems to be stuck up or elitist (If he talks nonstop about himself and how great he is), run away from him as quickly as you can! (And don't say to me, "But Grandpa, he was cute!")

CHAPTER 24:
Choices

"Walking with a friend in the dark is better than walking alone in the light."

– Helen Keller

Dear Lydia:

Every day of your life is filled with many choices you are required to make. Some of these choices are big. It might be choosing the college you want to attend, the guy you're going to marry, or the first house you're going to buy. You may struggle with choices and toss and turn in bed at night trying to decide, as I sometimes do. The indecision might bother you more than anything. As I have already told you, one reason I wrote this book was to help you understand yourself, a crucial step in life. One thing I have recently come to understand about myself is that I'm a processor. Given a little time to make decisions, my mind, especially my subconscious mind, will process the difficult choices, and eventually the answers will come to me.

Most choices in work life don't appear to be quite so monumental. They are the small decisions you make every day of your life. You choose what clothes to wear to school, what you want to eat from the menu at a restaurant, whether to stop when the light turns yellow, or whether to hit the snooze on your alarm and sleep just ten minutes longer in the morning before getting up and going to school. (When your mom was young, she was such a deep sleeper that she was practically impossible to awaken in the morning.) My point here is that sometimes choices may appear to be inconsequential, but in reality, they are big. Before I met your Grandma Becky when we were students at UW-Oshkosh, her cute, brown hair and the long, green coat caught my eye. I asked a nursing student friend if he knew her. He introduced me, and I asked her out. (On our first date, we went out for pizza and a movie, *Marathon Man*. I thought it was a movie about running. Instead, it was a thriller. I know, not very romantic.) Now, did that seemingly simple choice of buying and wearing that green coat mean we would fall in love and be married for over thirty-seven years? Probably not, but who knows?

Whenever I think of choices, I think about the decision to drive somewhere on Wisconsin roads during the winter especially if the forecast is calling for snow. "I will be careful" and "I will be fine" are two things fearful parents often hear when asked to borrow the car. In my first book, *Coaching Our Sons*, I related the tragic story of four boys from Spring Green, Wisconsin, who decided to see a movie in a neighboring town on a cold winter's night. On the way there, they skidded on treacherous black ice and hit a truck head-on. All four boys were killed. After that accident, I have wondered how quickly they came to that decision to go to that movie. You never know. Lydia, my advice to you is to be careful with choices, even the little choices, you make in life.

Your daily choices become your habits, and your habits become your life. I always prefer keeping my options open. For instance, it was never my dream or goal to become a coach. Throughout my life, as you have figured out by now, I have always loved sports: basketball, baseball, and football. At the same time, academics were always just as important. After becoming a teacher in 1979 in Plymouth, Wisconsin, I was also asked to coach basketball at the middle school level. To me, it was a great fit, teaching and coaching. (Although some educators may disagree with me, I believe that great coaches are great teachers.) I also had a love of history. I simply could not get enough of it. At the time, I read everything I could get my hands on about the Civil War, going to the Renaissance Book Store in Milwaukee to buy whatever I could find. Your Grandma Becky and I traveled out east to tour Gettysburg, Antietam, Chancellorsville, and other Civil War battlefields. (Because it was cheaper, we tent camped even though she was about six months pregnant with your Uncle Wes at the time. I gave her a lot of credit for that!) At that time, as I was teaching and pursuing my master's degree, a valued mentor advised me to consider getting a doctorate in history and teaching at the college level. I remember exactly where I was on the UW-Oshkosh campus when we had the conversation. I cannot remember, however, how or where I was when I made my decision. I didn't see it at the time, but it was a real fork in the road for my life and my children's lives. I chose not to do it. Instead, I stuck with teaching and coaching at the high school level. I have touched the lives of thousands. I have been fortunate enough to coach in five state tournaments, high school basketball's Holy Grail. Yet, even so, I look back and wonder if I made that huge decision in my life without enough thought.

You hear a lot today about basing choices and decisions on data. It has been said by some who claim to have more insight and knowledge than I do that we are a data-driven society, and all decisions should be based on data. It has been my experience, however, that data can be manipulated and especially when a lot of the data, but perhaps not all, favors the point which you are trying to make.

A second method of making decisions is through using your instinct or intuition. Data people frown upon this, but my advice to you is not to dismiss your intuition too quickly. I have seen some data people with seemingly good ideas crash and burn because their ideas went against the intuition of others. Your Great-Grandma Lydia Tank was someone who never graduated from high school, but she had great instincts. Near the end of my four years at UW-Oshkosh, I was finishing my coursework and dating your Grandma Becky, who graduated a semester ahead of me and was a nurse at St. Luke's Hospital in Milwaukee. Life was good in the spring of 1979, as I was getting ready to start my teaching job search. Suddenly out of nowhere, another woman in one of my classes showed an interest in me. I was totally surprised. The following weekend I went home to Sheboygan Falls to visit my parents and was feeling pretty good about myself. During previous months, I had already brought Becky back to Sheboygan Falls, and my parents liked her immediately. As I was growing up, I was fortunate to have a strong emotional connection with my mother. We talked a lot, were very close, and I could tell her anything. Well, without even thinking, I happened to mention that this other young woman had shown an interest in me. Great-Grandma Lydia, all one hundred pounds of her and not a healthy woman, immediately got up into my face and said in no uncertain terms that she did not want to hear this at all. "We like Becky!" she willfully asserted. My mom just knew. Her mother's intuition told her that your grandmother was the one for me, and she was right.

One last word of advice regarding choices and decision-making is to play to your strengths but improve your weaknesses. You decide what each is, and the first thing you must do is figure them out. Some people make the mistake of getting stuck on an emotional treadmill of their mistakes. You will conquer your dreams and climb your mountain if you can avoid that. You're choosing to succeed!

CHAPTER 25:
Control the Things You Can Control

> "When life gives you a hundred reasons to cry,
> show life that you have a thousand reasons to smile."
>
> – Source unknown

Dear Lydia:

Throughout your life different things, situations, and various people will frustrate you. Your Great-Grandfather Bill Tank would call drivers who made mistakes on the road "doughheads," and my brother Jon and I, riding in the backseat of the Rambler with our seatbelts unbuckled, would laugh. Or waiting behind another car at a stoplight that had already turned green, Bill would say, "Well, it's not going to get any greener!" They were simple comments he would make about people doing things over which he had no control.

Some people feel a greater need to be in control than others, and when even the simplest things over which they have no control occur, it bothers them more than it would others. They have trouble getting past it. For these people, this can be crippling. When this takes place in relationships, both people suffer. When it happens in the workplace, it becomes more difficult to do your job efficiently and effectively. My advice to you, Lydia, is to learn to let it go.

It can be easy to worry, and for some people, worrying is a choice they make. You will be happier and healthier if you develop your ability not to worry. Instead, the best thing to do is focus on the things you can control. Sometimes this is easier said than done. For instance, over the years I had great success as a basketball coach. As the years went by, I think I enjoyed the victories less, and the depths of the defeats tended to linger longer. As a result, I started to lose my focus on the things I could control as a coach. Instead, I started to see the numbers more, such as our record or how many points per game we were averaging in comparison to past successful teams. These thoughts were making me feel ill before games. The mental stress of coaching was getting to me. Instead of focusing on the things I could control, I was stressing about things beyond my control. Your mom and Aunt Alli could see the toll it was taking on me and urged me to retire from coaching basketball, which I did after thirty years.

Lydia, if you grow up to play basketball, which because of your mom and dad wouldn't surprise me, controlling what you can control can make the difference between winning and losing, and if you're not careful, it can work against you. I worked hard to become a good shooter in high school as did your mom, dad, and Uncle Wes. To become a very good shooter, you cannot worry if you miss shots. There is an old basketball adage that goes, "Shooters shoot to get hot, and shooters shoot to stay hot." Another is that "shooters have to have short memories." In other words, if you miss, forget it. You cannot control it. Instead, focus on the things over which you have a little more control such as how hard you work, rebounding, defense, and hustle. If you focus on those things, your shots will start to fall. But as I stated earlier, it's easier said than done.

Some coaches and teams are pretty good at getting into the heads of the players on other teams. One prominent Wisconsin high school basketball coach allowed his players to dunk during pregame warm-up drills until the officials came onto the court, something blatantly illegal but effective to intimidate an already intimidated opposing team. Other school officials allowed their students to taunt the opposing team. The television media encourages this when they show highlights of players yelling at their opponent after making a good play. Again, you cannot control the behavior of others. Focus on controlling what you can control.

The same is true for runners. It's difficult to mask it if you aren't as fast or if you haven't trained as well. You cannot control how fast another runner is, either on your team or the competition. You cannot control the weather. It might be too cold for most people to run, or it might be 95 degrees, a time when the mentally weak are looking for a cool dip in the pool or a shady spot to rest. You cannot control the weather, but you can control your attitude and your response to the weather. Likewise, I have always admired those athletes who could control their emotions.

What are things you can control in life? You can control how hard you work at something. If you are lazy or make excuses when things don't turn out as you would like, then expect similar results. It does seem like there are more things that are beyond your control. You cannot easily control your looks, although some people try very hard to do so. You cannot control what other people say about you. This is my strongest reason to stay away from social media during your middle and high school years. When you become a parent, you will have to gradually let go of controlling your child's behavior. For some, this may be most difficult.

Lydia, even in a small town like Dodgeville, Wisconsin, growing up in the 2020s, you will be exposed to many mean and hurtful things. You will hear people refer to others who you thought were their friends in the nastiest terms. Because you are a girl, you might hear someone put you down or make you feel bad. During her early elementary school years, your mom was at the age when she was determining the difference between a "good word" and a "bad word," and she overheard a girl referred to as a "b-word." Very quickly her ears perked up, and she looked up at me and asked if that was a bad word. I said that yes, it's a very bad word, and boys should never call girls that. I told her that if a boy at school ever called her that, she had my permission to go up and punch him as hard as she could. (When she was little, she was a solidly built girl, not yet the distance running champion she was to become.) Her eyes got big as she then asked me, "Wouldn't I get sent to the principal's office?" I told her that she might but just to tell them there that your dad said it was okay. Luckily, your mom never tested it out.

The underlying point is that you cannot control others around you. You can only control yourself, and as a girl, you should stand up for yourself. Don't accept sexism, homophobia, racism, or what I find to be the most recent plague in our society, ageism. (Check out how elderly people are made fun of in the media today or how people jokingly say, "Oh, you're just old.") In school, you may discover that certain teachers have their favorite students (other students are always aware), or how certain employers always seem to hire the cute girls. Even worse, those cute girls are encouraged to dress a certain way to get more tip money. You are fortunate to live in a time when this is not acceptable. It is a fine line, but control what you can control, and stand up for yourself when conditions are unacceptable.

CHAPTER 26:
Helping Others

"If you want to lift yourself up, lift up someone else."

– Booker T. Washington

Dear Lydia:

You are being raised in a world in which the gap between the wealthy and the people who struggle to get by is steadily increasing. The ability to improve one's lot in life by going from a lower social class to a higher one, which was once what America was about, is more difficult now than ever before. This began quietly during the decade of the 1980s, which has gone down in history as the "Age of Greed" in America. It was an era of decadent living in which the growing norm for many Americans was to care only about themselves and less about giving back to others or helping others less fortunate. At the time, I did not know or understand this at all. I was newly married and still trying to figure out life as a teacher, coach, husband, and father. I did not see the big picture. Today, more than a generation has passed since the 1980s, and there are still many people whose goal is to live this way. They care only about themselves. Lydia, my advice to you is to reject this way of thinking.

When I was growing up in Sheboygan Falls, I never knew, although I should have, that money was tight in our family even before the many medical issues set in. Your Great-Grandfather Bill Tank and Great-Grandmother Lydia Tank not only worked hard to raise their family, they did a good job of keeping their financial struggles from us. For me, Christmas was the most looked forward to holiday. Every year my dad would tell us with a straight face that this year there would not be much under the Christmas tree. Every year I believed him, and every year there were a number of gifts for the children. My parents, however, only got one gift for each other. They couldn't afford it, so the emphasis was on making the kids happy. I will never forget that.

When I went off to college, perhaps sensing subconsciously that because of their health issues my time with my parents was running out, I wondered what I could do to repay them for their many years of sacrifice for me. In the spring of 1979, my parents, your great-grandparents, proudly drove to the campus to attend my graduation ceremony at the Kolf Sports Center. Because I knew that an overnight stay in a motel could stretch their budget, I had made a motel reservation in Oshkosh and paid for their night's stay there. At the time, it was a small thing, but I look back on it today and feel good about it.

Lydia Tank was a woman wise beyond her years. She relayed another concept to me that did not make much sense at the time, but it does now, and I often think about it. As I was graduating from college and just before I married your Grandma Becky, I think Lydia knew better than I did that her time on earth was limited. Perhaps looking at the future and knowing that I had my whole adult life ahead of me, she took me aside for one of our many talks we had over the years. While I felt a sense of gratitude to her for all the years of sacrifice and a need to repay her in some way, she did not see it that way at all. Her advice to me, which I am now handing down to you, Lydia, is to someday pay it forward. I have never forgotten this advice, and I have used it in raising my own three children. The best way to repay someone is to do something nice for my kids and to help others in need.

Some people take the concept of helping others to a higher level. Over recent years at Dodgeville High School, a generous anonymous donor has given money during the holiday season to be disbursed to children from families in economic need throughout the four schools in the Dodgeville School District. I do not know who the donor is. He has chosen to remain anonymous, which I think is the coolest thing. I believe that the people who ask for nothing in return should feel the best. Many children in the district have been given money and taken to area stores to purchase gifts of their choice. Perhaps the best part of the story is that the majority of them did not buy anything for themselves. Instead, they chose to buy gifts for their siblings and parents. They chose to give rather than take. To me, this is contrary to the Age of Greed, and my hat is off to them.

    Don't be surprised that there are some people in great need who feel like they are being given handouts and will refuse anything you may want to do for them or give to them. They may even be insulted if you attempt to do so. They have the right to feel any way they want. You should respect their feelings, although you may want to tell them that if they reconsider, the offer still stands. When given that response I simply say that it's okay and I respect their decision. It is not my intent to make them feel bad. I just enjoy helping others.

    Some people feel like failures, and even worse, they feel like they are being judged by others as failures. It is very important for you not to judge people or allow them to feel judged in any way. Like the 1950s television hero the Lone Ranger who, after solving a crime and helping someone out, would quietly vanish from the scene. Hence the perpetual final line of each television episode, often spoken by a beautiful woman whom he rescued: "And we didn't even get to thank him." After helping someone, don't wait around for the praise. If they feel the need to say thank you, simply say, "You're welcome."

    The little things you do to help people are perhaps just as important as the big things. Notice how you feel when you hold a door open for someone and allow them to enter before you. (As a girl, you may not do this as much. Do take note, however, if a boy does this for you! If he does it for you on the first date, that's good. If he almost always does it, even better.) This act of kindness shows great respect for older people or people who have difficulty walking, especially someone with a walker. Most often these people are very grateful. If they're not, then they may be entitled!

    What other little things can you do to help people? A vanishing sight in small-town Wisconsin is the child-run Kool-Aid or lemonade stand. As a boy in Sheboygan Falls, I set up Kool-Aid stands on the corner of Cherry Street and Fond du Lac Avenue, which was then Highway 23, and attempted to ply my trade. I never made much money at it, but I was always so appreciative when drivers would pull over and buy a cup of Kool-Aid. Today, I try to pay it forward. Every time I see kids selling cool drinks, I stop and buy some. They probably think I'm being a nice guy for buying one of their drinks, but in my mind, I'm just thinking back to the early 1960s, and I'm thanking those kind people who helped me out.

CHAPTER 27:
Being Stubborn

"Champions keep playing until they get it right."

– Billie Jean King

Dear Lydia:

Admittedly, I am the self-reported king of being stubborn. When I was young, the term was "bullheaded." Your Grandma Becky has called me a stubborn German, and she is absolutely correct. It's who I am, and as such, it is part of my blood. Of course, your Grandma Becky is very proud of her Irish heritage, which has also been passed down to you. As parents, she and I have noticed in our three children evidence of that German stubbornness as well as the Irish temper. For you, I guess you have the best of both worlds along with the Scandinavian traits from your dad's Alleman side.

Since early childhood, your mother has been the same way. She's a bulldog if she wants something bad enough. This is especially true if she feels like she has been wronged or mistreated by someone. If that is the case, that stubbornness goes into overdrive. Don't even try to change her mind. You're fighting a losing battle. There is an old saying that "still waters run deep." In some ways, that's what this is saying. Once your mom has made up her mind, it's over, and that's just the way it's going to be.

I have watched you grow and develop from your birth through your first birthday. It seems like every week you are growing physically and learning daily. As your grandpa, I am fascinated, and it has been a delight to watch you learn. I see that stubborn quality emerging in you just as it did in your mother. You get very angry when you don't get your way. And you let everyone know it. For instance, getting you into a sleep schedule, either in the evening or during naptimes, could be a problem even when you were tired and in need of sleep. We felt that you really did not want to miss any of the action. You especially enjoyed all the attention you were getting, being the first grandchild on both sides of the family. When it was time for you to sleep, your mom fed you your last bottle and rocked you as you felt your soft blanket and started to doze. As she put you in your crib in the darkened room with a fan on for white noise, she put a pacifier in your mouth. On more than one occasion, you got mad. You took the nook out of your mouth and threw it across the room as if to say, "Take that!" We quickly came to distinguish your mad cry from your tired cry or your hungry cry. You also liked to move around without restraint. You fought the necessity of being put into your car seat. When you first threw your nook, and when you arched your back in an attempt to stay out of your car seat, it was then that I knew I had seen the stubborn Lydia. Welcome to the family!

Being stubborn is not always a bad thing. If you can harness it, your stubbornness can be what turns you into a great athlete or musician or student. Being stubborn is another way of saying that you are strong-willed. This can be viewed as a strength. My advice to you is to turn a potential weakness into what could become your defining strength. Establish the "refuse to lose" attitude as an athlete. Similarly, you have heard coaches say, "Never quit!" or "Never give up!" (There comes the point in nearly every athletic competition when the team or person who is behind starts looking at the scoreboard and wonders if the game is over. Their effort drops off, and some just go through the motions until the end of the contest.)

As I said, success in sports is not all about the glitz and glitter. When your teammates make a good play and then proceed to play it up to their friends in the stands, don't follow their example. Just make the play and then go and make the next one without emotion. Remember, the best athletes in any sport do not like to lose. When opponents start to say that about you, then you are more than halfway down the road to beating them. A good attitude is such an important quality to have!

Your mom was an eight-time Division III All-American in track and field at UW-Platteville. As I said, she had that "refuse to lose" attitude. She used that stubborn streak in a positive way. High school track and field Coach Joe Hanson saw that attitude as a source of strength in Ann. As her daughter, however, you will make your own way. Coach Hanson relayed some excellent advice that legendary and Hall of Fame track and field Coach Bill Gritton once gave him. "The runners are not you. You're not running anymore. You're not coaching you. You're coaching her. If you remember anything, remember that they're not you." Great advice.

On the other hand, your mom's best races were always after she had run an earlier event and not done as well as she would've liked. It wasn't anything anyone ever had to say to her. Her stubbornness just seemed to kick in.

CHAPTER 28:
Eating

*"Eat to live,
don't live to eat."*

– Benjamin Franklin

Dear Lydia:

It has been said by the esteemed early American Founding Father Benjamin Franklin in his *Poor Richard's Almanac*, a collection of sage-like sayings that Americans should "Eat to live, don't live to eat." Today, well over 200 years later with obesity an epidemic, few people are listening to his advice. We have become a nation of people who consume gluttonous portions of food at every meal. What we eat is not always healthy either. Your Grandma Becky is a cardiac rehabilitation nurse and would be better suited than I am to give you advice on this topic. She is deluged daily with people who deal with heart-related issues and how they can correct them. She is the expert, and most of her patients revere her.

As you know, my mother's parents were early 1900s German immigrants who settled in Kohler, Wisconsin. Like thousands of immigrants at that time, Gottlieb Seidenzahl worked at the Kohler Company and with his new bride went on to raise their five children in that village. From what I was told, they enjoyed eating. Food was plentiful, and your Great-Grandmother Lydia was given various recipes for many calorie-rich foods, most of which have been lost through the generations. During frequent Seidenzahl gatherings of the 1950s and 1960s, there was always a lot of food and some of the most delicious German desserts ever made. (Unfortunately, I never knew my Grandfather Gottlieb, who passed away in 1954, and Emma died six years later when I was only four.) Before I go any further, my advice to you is to get the recipe for blitz torte handed down from your Great-Grandma Lydia Tank to your Grandma Becky. To make it is a very tedious and time-consuming procedure, but it's my favorite. (It must be a very special occasion for me to get a blitz torte. When I do get it, I don't share it easily, although I shared it with you when I recently turned 61, and you seemed to enjoy every bite. If you're lucky enough to have your mom make it for you, get your fair share because it won't last.)

For some people, eating is an emotional event. (Not for me. I enjoy good food, but I don't get emotional about it, although it's close with a good cheeseburger or a rare brat.) Surprisingly, because of how skinny she is, your mom has always loved to eat good food. When Aunt Alli and your mom were toddlers, your Grandma Becky would take them to play dates with other mothers of young children. They were social events meant to get everyone out of the house and allow the little ones to learn to play together. Everyone enjoyed themselves. There were always good snacks set out. As everyone gathered, and the children greeted each other with smiles and hugs, your mom became well known for heading directly to the snack area and sampling the food. Your Grandma Becky felt compelled to explain that yes, your mom had eaten breakfast earlier that morning.

When your mom was a young girl, your Grandma Becky often worked the second shift from 3 to 11 p.m. She and I thought it was a good thing because then our three kids would only be at daycare for a minimal amount of time, perhaps from 2:30 p.m. until 4 or 5 p.m. depending on if I was coaching basketball or not. (As they got older, they would go to the high school gym during my practice. Even then they would go to my classroom and scavenge for candy.) Invariably, when I picked them up, they were all hungry. They also knew that I didn't cook, and your Grandma Becky prepared all the meals ahead of time. All I had to do was microwave them. On one occasion, they asked me what we were having for dinner as we made our way home. There was one particularly healthy and tasty meal made up of rice, chicken, and broccoli called "chicken no peek," and when I told them that their mom had made that for us, they begged me in unison, "Please, Dad, not that. Can we just go to McDonald's? Dad, please, we won't tell Mom!" (As most children do, they knew my weakness, and it was Big Macs at the time). Although I was tempted, I did not cave in to their demands. We ate the chicken no peek that night. The irony is that as adults, they all enjoy chicken no peek and sometimes even ask for it. (One of the first adult foods you ate was chicken no peek. You liked it.)

I think you take after your mother. Seeing you first as a baby and now as a toddler, it is fun to watch you get excited when you think you are about to eat. As an infant, you quickly became attuned to the sound of the microwave being turned on. If food or a bottle was being prepared for you, the excitement in you would build as you would wave your arms back and forth and up and down until whatever was on the menu arrived. This continued as a toddler when you would point and say, "mmmm" and then smack your lips as your food was arriving. Also, much to your mother's dismay, you would spit out foods you didn't like as much such as certain vegetables. Your mom and dad quickly learned to disguise the taste of the vegetables by giving them with things you did like.

My advice to you is to eat healthy. Eat other foods but only in moderation. One of your Grandma Becky's favorite sayings to our three kids when they were growing up as they loved eating chips and snacks, something I am sorry to say they probably got from me, was, "You're going to get sick!" I don't think anyone ever did, with only one exception. At one family gathering, your Aunt Alli ate nearly an entire tray of chocolate brownies and later complained of having a stomachache. As healthy as your Grandma Becky tries to eat, one of her few weaknesses is Oreo cookies. She says that they are her kryptonite as her willpower against them melts away. She has been known to consume entire rows of Oreos within the blink of an eye. Of course, I am not allowed to have them in the house. When I bought my first small package of Oreos for you and thought I put them in your "secret place," they somehow disappeared. Lydia, eat healthy and get exercise as I know you will, and I believe you will live a long life. However, and I believe that even the great Ben Franklin would agree, don't forget my advice about the blitz torte!

CHAPTER 29:
Time

> *"One of the lessons that I grew up with was to always stay true to yourself and never let what somebody else says distract you from your goals. And so when I hear about negative and false attacks, I really don't invest any energy in them because I know who I am."*
>
> – Michelle Obama

Dear Lydia:

At some point when you are a young girl, you will gain a sense of time. At times, it will even seem to stand still. During the sultry summer months of your elementary school years, time will seem endless. You might sleep late on some mornings or play outside with friends well after the sun has set. Your mom might even tell you that it's time for you to go to bed, but you will wonder why? Tomorrow is just another day. If you are especially perceptive, you might even notice that your mom, dad, and grandparents appear to be getting older. You won't really care though because it seems like time affects other people but not yourself. Your world as you know it has not changed. At some point, you might even think that you have an infinite amount of time. You don't.

There is nothing like having a grandchild to give anyone a sense of their mortality along with the knowledge that the clock is ticking. Every time I see you I see change and development. I felt a pang of sadness along with joy recently when I watched you take your first unaided steps. Appropriately, it was on my backyard basketball court. There was pride and happiness on your face as we cheered you on. You had displayed the courage and succeeded. Your babyhood was now officially over, and your toddler years had begun. To me, I wanted to say no, not yet. Don't let her grow up yet. In the words of some wise sage somewhere: "Time waits for no one."

Value your time and don't waste it. As you grow, you will hear that time goes by very quickly. Believe it. Then multiply that by about one hundred. That's how fast time goes by. In church, you will often hear talk of eternity. That is forever without end. It is difficult to even imagine what that concept means. It is also said that your life here on earth, even if you live well into your eighties, is only a tiny fraction of eternity.

I feel the clock ticking, as I turned 61 years old this past year. While I do not have a death wish for myself, I am realistic enough to understand that I am not going to live forever and my time could be up sooner rather than later. It is the primary reason that I am writing *Letters to Lydia*. I want you and my other grandchildren to have a good understanding of who I am and then who you are. That said, hopefully I spend many years with you and you get to know me firsthand. If, however, I am not there at some point in your life, please understand that it's not because I don't want to be there.

When I tell people how many books I read each year, or that I try to exercise each day, or that I like to spend some time each day in reflection just thinking or planning, a common response I hear is, "Oh, I just don't have time for that." I understand. During the busiest times of my life when I coached basketball, I spent much of my time scouting either in person or from film, doing stats from film, strategizing for the next game, practicing, fundraising, or talking to concerned parents about why their son wasn't playing as much as they had envisioned. Meanwhile, I was also preparing for what I was going to teach the following day in my history classes. I also had to make time to be a father as well as a husband. I still tried to find time to read books, exercise daily, and think. Remember that what you do becomes your habits, and your habits become who you are as a person. So my advice to you as well as to those people who make excuses about not having enough time to do some of those things which they know they should do and want to do is to prioritize and then find a way because it can be done.

I am in my thirty-ninth year of teaching history. On the first day of class each year, I tell the students that there are three reasons to study and learn history. The first reason, which they have all heard since they were young, and I believe to be the worst of the three, is so they don't repeat the mistakes of the past. (I ask them to compare the American Revolution in which thirteen disunited colonies fought the most powerful British Empire to the war in Vietnam in which the small communist country defeated the United States.) The second reason is so they have a better understanding of themselves and the world around them. What motivated someone to do something a hundred years ago? What was the life expectancy of the average American a hundred years ago? The third reason is perhaps the one I like the best. It is the most common reason that the light bulb goes on over the heads of my students. I want students to see that the way things are today aren't the way things have always been. (At this point, I ask them how long will it be until high school students don't have any concept of what a landline telephone is.)

Certainly, I see the value of studying history. It is my passion in life, and since those days back in the 1970s of learning the wisdom of Dr. Watson Parker, I have loved history. History is the passage of time. However, my advice to you, Lydia, is that while you study the past, try to stay in the present, but prepare for the future. When you don't have that foundation on which to build your house, your house will crumble.

Friday afternoon classes at Dodgeville High School can drag on for students. The clocks on the walls appear to be moving in slow motion. At times, it seems like they don't even move. If you're an athlete and you have a game or a meet that night, the pregame nerves may begin to set in. If you're a runner, you may ask your teacher to go fill up your water bottle every fifteen minutes because of your need to hydrate and then, of course, go to the bathroom because of all the water you drank. Hopefully, you have given some thought to organizing and prioritizing your homework for the weekend. Maybe you will even have an after-school job. The clock has finally moved. It is 3:25 p.m. You may leave. Hooray! The weekend is finally here! You either go to your sports practice, your game, walk home, or you get a ride home from your boyfriend, Elmer. You love the weekend and your time off. One quick word of advice, though, regarding time. Sleeping in on the weekend, although it feels good, does make the weekend go faster. If you value your time and want the weekend to last longer, get up early on Saturday and Sunday.

CHAPTER 30:
Drinking and Drugs

"Drinking and driving: there are stupider things, but it's a very short list."

– Author unknown

Dear Lydia:

Sooner or later, everyone is confronted with the decision of whether or not to drink alcohol or try some mood-altering drug. By the time you are in middle school, you will hear rumors that some of your classmates are smoking, and others have already moved on to beer, wine, or marijuana. At first, when you hear this, you might be a little shocked. Perhaps one of your good friends might even try to tempt you with something, or a cute boy you have been anxious to connect with offers you something, which you know is wrong. You want to fit in. In some ways, you already feel different from your friends, and even some teachers treat you differently because both of your parents are teachers. When you're in high school, the issue is still there, although it is no longer new. More of your friends and classmates go to parties where alcohol is readily available. Yet you resist. Because of who your parents are, some friends drift away from you and form other social groups from which you are excluded. You become annoyed when teammates on your sports teams give in to the peer pressure and start drinking during the season, and the coaches talk about what "phenomenal kids" they have the pleasure to work with on this year's team. You read it in the local newspaper, and you hear it repeated at the end of the year banquet. It might even become an "invisible elephant in the room" and cause team dynamics to change (more about invisible elephants in a later chapter). The unfairness of it makes you feel frustrated and angry.

When you go through that and make the choice of whether to drink or not, or whether or not to use a mood-altering substance, the first thing I want to tell you is that I understand what you are going through because I have been there. Your Great-Grandma Lydia Tank was raised in a family in which alcohol was a problem. As a girl in Kohler, she saw her father, Gottlieb Seidenzahl, taken to an alcohol rehab hospital in Oshkosh to "dry out." Because of that, she never drank, and she instilled (no pun intended) in us a fear of alcohol. So, alcoholism is a part of your family history. The only alcohol my dad drank was the one can of Old Milwaukee beer when he grilled brats on Sundays at noon. Because I took what she had to say to heart, I never drank throughout high school or college. Teammates on my state championship teams were caught and punished for drinking. Although I am sure now that I wasn't, at the time I felt like the only student at UW-Oshkosh, a known "party school" during the late 1970s, who did not drink or use there. When a good friend on my floor in the dorm offered to share his stash of marijuana with me, I just said, "No, thanks." Like in high school, I felt very alone.

Your mom and Aunt Alli said similar things about their high school days. As you move closer to graduation, it can be worse. They spent many Saturday nights at home while their friends were out having a good time. Luckily, though, at least they had each other. To many people, your mom and Aunt Alli were known as "the girls." They were well known locally, and some people still ask about them even though your mom has returned to Dodgeville. As "the girls," they had each other to lean on for extra support.

My advice to you, Lydia, is to always talk to your mom and dad about your feelings. Lean on them. Use their insight. If you are feeling pressured, talk to them about it. Don't wait for them to naturally know what you're feeling without you telling them. When you go off to college, have a plan for how to handle drinking. Are you going to drink? If so, how much? This might be the biggest decision you make over your four years. Don't make this decision lightly. It's understandable that you will want to fit in and be part of a social group. However, if you decide to drink at college, three things can happen, and two of them are pretty bad. First, you might drink and have a fun time with your friends, and that might be all. By far, most kids who eventually become problem drinkers either during high school, college, or after graduation think this will be them. Second, you slowly develop a severe drinking problem. You cannot wait until your next drink. It starts to interfere with other areas of your life. Third, you become an alcoholic, someone who is addicted to the high of alcohol. I could even add a fourth, which is the greatest number of date rapes on college campuses involve heavy alcohol use. In extreme cases of alcohol use on college campuses, every parent's worst nightmare, drinking can result in overdose or death. Lydia, am I trying to scare you? Yes, of course I am. Perhaps the most important words of advice from a grandfather to his grandchildren are, "Be careful!"

And then there is drinking and driving. Every time you choose to get behind the wheel of a car after you have been drinking or in a car with a friend who has been drinking, you are playing Russian roulette with your life. However, the weapon of choice is a car rather than a gun. Before you even think about doing that, pause and imagine the police ringing your mom and dad's doorbell at 2 a.m. Imagine the look of agonizing pain on your mom's and dad's faces as they are given the news that their daughter, Lydia, has just been killed in a crash involving alcohol. Imagine the agony felt by your grandfather, Chuck Tank, as he delivers your eulogy, something so difficult, he could have barely imagined it.

Okay, Lydia, go ahead and say it. I know that as you have been reading this chapter, you are probably thinking that you have seen me drinking beer. You know that your mom loves Leinenkugel's Summer Shandy, and your dad prefers New Glarus Spotted Cow. My response to you is that when you are of legal age, you will be welcome to come over to my house like your parents do and have a beer. In the German culture, there is the term gemutlichkeit. In essence, it means people are sitting around hashing out issues in a friendly way over a keg of beer on a hot Sunday afternoon. To me, that sounds perfect. I think there has been a bit of gemutlichkeit handed down through the generations to me from my Grandfather Gottlieb Seidenzahl. It is part of my German heritage. Do I abuse alcohol? Do I drink until I'm plastered? No. Do I drink hard alcohol? Rarely. Do I enjoy having a beer? Absolutely.

CHAPTER 31:

Priorities

"When I stand before God at the end of my life, I would hope that I would not have a single bit of talent left, and could say, 'I used everything you gave me.'"

– Erma Bombeck

Dear Lydia:

You will probably feel stress at different times in your life because you have too much on your plate. If you're a runner like your parents, you have to get your daily miles in to prepare for the next race or season. If you are a basketball player, you have to practice your shot or play in endless tournament games. If you have a job, your boss says you should not be late for work. And, of course, if you are in high school, you are hearing the constant barrage of teachers and counselors telling you about the importance of grades and class rank to prepare for and get accepted into the college of your choice. Yes, there is pressure on you to succeed. You might even have an occasional meltdown because it all becomes too much for you to handle. This is normal, and you're not the only one to feel the stress (hopefully not in second grade!).

My first piece of advice in this regard is to your mother. In today's era of "helicopter parenting," a parent's first impulse is to do whatever she can to rescue her child. If you got your first "B," or (heaven forbid) a "C" on an Advanced Placement quiz, she is likely to share your stress. She might ask how she can help you in the class. (Hopefully, she has not been helping you extensively or even doing your homework for you as you have gone on in school.) To her, my advice is, "Don't panic." Give necessary support to Lydia throughout this growth process. Keep repeating my long-standing mantra, "It will be okay."

To you, my advice is to calmly reevaluate what you are doing. What caused you to feel this way, and how can YOU make it better? The best thing to do in this case is to firmly establish your priorities. These are the things that take precedence over everything else. When more than one priority is involved, how can you prioritize them? It is my experience as a teacher that kids today are often not taught how to establish their priorities. They are used to someone rescuing them. They may disagree with me there because they think they understand how to set their priorities. As I have said in previous chapters, I think it helps to write them down. Put them up on your wall or bathroom mirror next to the picture of your boyfriend, Elmer. They will be clearer in your mind if you look at them every day.

Even better, before you run into a personal crisis, sit down and talk to a personal mentor, someone whose opinion you value, and ask them what their top five priorities in life are. What are their top ten? Have they thought about them? For example, their priorities might be work, family, running, church, and friends. Have them explain to you how they arrived at their top five and why they are in the order they are. If they can give you a good explanation, then you are talking to someone who probably has their life on a good path. When you reach the point in your life where you are ready to find someone with whom you want to spend the next fifty years, ask him what his priorities in life are. Does he even know? How do they match up with your priorities?

I want to reiterate how important it is for you to walk the talk in life. If you say that something is your main priority, then your actions must show it. How can anyone say that they are living a

Jesus Christ centered life and then swear constantly or talk behind people's backs? How can a parent say that their family means more to them than anything and is their number one priority and then work long hours during the week before spending their weekends on the golf course? How can a high school basketball star tell everyone they profess to be "team first and me second," and then pout during a game when their teammate is scoring more points than they are? When you read these examples, they probably make sense to you. A lot of people say one thing but do another. Perhaps you have already seen people doing some of them. First of all, try not to judge other people. Second, do what is right for yourself, although when your mom tells you to clean your room, don't say to her, "Well, Grandpa says I should work on my priorities, and Mom, a clean room is really not my priority."

"You do what you have to do so that you can do what you want to do" is a good expression. Although it might not be your priority to shovel the snow from your driveway, it needs to be done to get to school in the morning. You might not like doing your science homework, but getting a good grade in Chemistry is important to graduate and go to college. Many kids in high school today either reject this way of thinking or choose to ignore it. Perhaps they regret it later.

CHAPTER 32:
Money

"Never spend your money before you have it."

– Thomas Jefferson

Dear Lydia:

For many people who make money, it is one of their biggest priorities. You will devote one third or more of your adult life earning a living at your job. Money is often one of the biggest stressors on relationships and a leading cause of divorce. How you learn to handle money, and how much income you have as an adult are two things that can have a direct impact on your happiness. Some people just cannot get enough of it. Politically, the gap between those people who possess tremendous amounts of money but want even more and those who barely get by widens daily. Many people who have lived without a lot of money may have referred to the old saying, "Money can't buy happiness, but it can sure help!"

Many people believe that the amount of money you have, which directly relates to the amount of stuff you own, determines how successful you are. I am not wealthy, although I live a happy life in the wealthiest country in the world. At some point, you may have to answer the question, "How much money do I really need?" A related question you will also need answer is, "What is the difference between what I want and what I need?" People who struggle with answering that question are often the same people who become obsessed with a shirt either at a store or online and must buy it. Then three days after buying it they have forgotten about it. It hangs in their closet, and they have moved on to the next thing that they have to have. So, ask yourself, "How much do I really need?"

When you grow up without the luxury of having a lot of extra money to spend, you learn the value of a dollar and the importance of saving. Some people are better savers than others. Some people can't spend their money quick enough. My dad, Bill Tank, used to say, "Don't be penny wise and dollar foolish." In some way, I think he was trying to tell me to be cautious with how I spent my money. When I was in middle school in 1969, I decided to save up and buy a new bicycle for myself. It was bright shiny green with a banana seat and butterfly handlebars. It cost $30, which for me at the time was so much that it might as well have been $500. I saved every penny I could get, did odd jobs, and mowed lawns for anyone who needed extra help. Every few days or so I emptied the cup of its dollars and coins and counted how much I had saved. I was very motivated. After two or three months, the big day came. Your Great-Grandpa Bill Tank took me to Sheboygan, and we bought the bike. What I recall most, however, is that we brought it home, and within a day the handlebars broke. Luckily my dad helped me return it, and I got a different new bike.

Buying your first car is a rite of passage. My dad told all four of his sons that they would each have to buy their own car. His thinking was that, not only could he not afford to buy us each a car, but we would take better care of it if we paid for it ourselves. So, like my middle school days saving for the bike, I saved money for a car in high school and college. Throughout my early college years when I would have to get rides from a friend or my dad to and from Sheboygan Falls and Oshkosh (your Great-Grandma Lydia never had a driver's license), I felt a little embarrassed as I watched my friends drive their cars. (Perhaps this explains my desire later in life to buy sports cars: four Mustangs and three Camaros.) By 1978, as I entered my senior year in college, I had saved $1,500. My dad and I went out and bought a brown, four-cylinder, four-year-old 1974 Ford Pinto for exactly $1,500. (Yes, I know. Because of the location of its gas tank, it was later said to be a death trap and would potentially explode when involved in rear collisions.) It was my first car. My dad was right. Because I bought it with my own money, I loved that car.

Perhaps my most important piece of advice to you involving your decision-making with money is to, when at all possible, avoid debt. I haven't always understood that. Actually, no one ever emphasized that to me. There were times during our marriage when your Grandma Becky and I had several bank credit cards, a number of store credit cards, two car loans, a home mortgage, and a bank line of credit on which we owed nearly $15,000. The interest alone on that last one was $70 a month. Together we decided that we needed to change our spending habits, and we got aggressive with paying off our debts. We also got all three of our children through college without any debt. Remember, good debt includes home mortgage and education. Bad debt includes credit cards, car loans, and Christmas shopping.

Lydia, even when you're young, save, save, save. As you grow older, treat saving like a bill. Set a little bit aside every week. Most people live paycheck to paycheck. When you get paid, try not to spend it all the first weekend. Keep track of your benefits, especially if you change jobs or careers. Also, don't forget the advice from the last chapter, "You do what you have to do so you can do what you want to do."

One of your Grandma Becky's and my favorite films came out in 1979, the year we were married. It's the Academy Award-winning film *Kramer vs. Kramer* starring Dustin Hoffman and Meryl Streep. It is the story of a young workaholic man whose wife leaves their young son and him. Over time, both the father and son work through major challenges and become much closer emotionally. The boy obviously misses his mother and the comfort of their routine. The father, an advertising agent who is used to devoting all of his time to his career, now must balance the roles of father and mother along with handling an increased workload at work. His priorities change as the film evolves. By the end of the movie, it has become clear that his career and money take a back seat to raising his son. If you ask most people which is more important, family or money, most people would probably say that their family is most important to them. If you dig deeper and look at their lifestyle and all their daily decisions, many people choose money over family. This is a mistake. As you marry and begin having your own children, take a step back and see which side of the coin you are on.

CHAPTER 33:

Invisible Elephant in the Room

"Fear less, hope more; eat less, chew more; whine less, breathe more; talk less, say more; hate less, love more; and all good things are yours."

– Swedish proverb

Dear Lydia:

This chapter is one which I considered not writing and is possibly my least favorite chapter to write. However, after giving it a fair amount of thought, I decided to anyway because it is a topic that you should consider. This topic has ruptured relationships. It has caused people to feel anguish. It's about issues that can dominate all types of relationships. Everyone knows the issue and can see it clearly. It's there in its dominating form, yet few people talk about it. If they are unable to contain themselves, and they do talk about it, it's almost never with the person most affected by it. It has also been said that people who say whatever they want whenever they want because they have no filter are always getting themselves into trouble because of this. To them, the topic is open for discussion. However, if you have a clear understanding of your priorities, this topic might have a direct impact on then. It's known as the invisible elephant in the room.

As you know by now, when I was in high school and college, I was driven to get the best grades. I wanted only "A"s and worked very hard to achieve a high grade point average. When I was a freshman at UW-Oshkosh, one of the most difficult courses I took was a history course called Ancient Civilizations. When I came into the class, I had only a minimal background in world history. I knew I would have my hands full, but I was determined to do well. The professor who taught the course was an elderly and kindly man who seemed to have health issues. His eyesight was failing him, and he frequently would lose his train of thought mid-sentence of a lecture. It quickly became apparent to me that in this class if I wanted to understand the seemingly endless line of ancient Egyptian pharaohs and the rulers of ancient Rome, I would have to study a lot on my own.

Then there was a friend in my dorm who also happened to be in the same class. He was from a town not too far from Sheboygan Falls, and we both enjoyed basketball. We sat next to each other in the class, although at least once or twice a week he skipped the early morning history class, making one excuse or another. Although the classroom was small, we sat in the back row, and at least I tried hard to listen and learn. My friend, however, rarely studied. In other classes that required papers to be written, he simply had his older sister write them for him. But, the invisible elephant in the room was that on exam days, he would sit next to me with his textbook open on his lap during the test! He blatantly cheated, and the professor who couldn't see very well never caught him. In all the history courses I took in my undergraduate and graduate programs, this was the only class in which I received a "B." My friend got an "A." Today, there is a fair amount of cheating that goes on in school. Some kids are proud and even brag about it. Other kids know who cheats and who doesn't. It is the invisible elephant in the room.

It is most common for people to ignore invisible elephants, although, on more than one occasion, a student has quietly informed me after taking an exam that another student cheated. Most often, I already knew and had taken steps to deal with it. Most families also have a fair number of invisible elephants. As you will see in an upcoming chapter, family traditions help kids build and understand who they are, but invisible elephants within the family hurt that. It is my theory that the more invisible elephants that are present within families, the more communication breakdowns there are, which cause emotional walls to be built. If a student is going to be successful in school, emotional walls need to be dissolved.

Your Grandma Becky descends from a proud Irish-American family. Her surprise trip to Ireland for our thirty-fifth wedding anniversary was a trip of a lifetime. However, for centuries the Irish have been notorious drinkers. For many families today, alcohol is an invisible elephant in the room passed down through generations.

So, Lydia, what should you do when you're confronted with an invisible elephant? I don't have any standard bit of advice here. Should you expose the elephant by talking about it to the group, or should you simply let it go? Go with your own intuition. Again, talk to a mentor about what to do. Just know that everyone faces invisible elephants. You're not alone.

CHAPTER 34:
Little Things

"I may not be there yet, but I'm closer than I was yesterday."

– Author unknown

Dear Lydia:

Throughout life, I have come to believe that if you take care of the little things, the big things take care of themselves. When you give thought to the little things that make up your life, eventually live your life within routines, and the patterns build connections. If you don't build those connections and routines, then you become frustrated because it seems like you are wandering aimlessly through your life. Every day is different, which may not seem all that bad, but you may be going about your daily business randomly. You are probably repeating things. As I have advised you on other things, ask someone you trust what the five most important little things in their life are. You may already have several of them on your list, but there will probably be at least one you hadn't considered on there, which could be a difference maker for you.

I like writing lists. Writing things down helps me organize and prioritize tasks when I have a lot I need or want to do. My suggestion to you is that when you have created a list of things to do, do the things on the list first that you dislike the most. When you get that done, you will be surprised at how much better you feel because it's out of the way. Doing the other things then becomes easier.

There is a saying in sports that "Practice makes perfect." Many parents have happily watched as their son or daughter practiced in the driveway, court, or on a playground, not understanding that they were watching them do things the wrong way. Perhaps they had seen some brief highlights from a game, and now they were trying to emulate what they saw instead of trying to perfect the necessary skills. That sports saying should be, "Perfect practice makes perfect." As a basketball coach, I tried to build small habits into my players: when to shoot, dribble, or pass the ball for instance. As time went on, that little thing became a habit, and that habit led to success. I was teaching them how to play the game instead of teaching them plays.

Seemingly the smallest things can become big things very quickly. A few years ago, a college cross country teammate of your Aunt Alli and your mom was killed in a tragic car accident. While she was stopped in traffic on a busy highway waiting to make a left turn, she may have turned her steering wheel too soon. A distracted truck driver following her struck her car from behind, sending her car into an oncoming car. Sadly, the beautiful and talented young woman with her life in front of her was killed in the collision. So, Lydia, while you're stopped in traffic, don't turn your steering wheel before making a turn. On a related driving note, never text or check your phone while driving, even when you're stopped at a red light. Better yet, don't have your phone within reach while you're driving. These are little things, but little things can lead to big things.

Learning how to keep things in perspective is a good way to help prevent small issues from becoming big issues. Additionally, I always try to remember that bad things are usually not that bad, and good things are not as good as they seem to be. While you should maintain that "refuse to lose" attitude, at the same time, don't get too excited when you win or too down when you lose. Learn from bad things and move on.

What are some little things that have served me well and can make a difference?

- Always put your keys and your wallet in the same spot whenever you are at home, work, or school.
- Give food to people, especially those who really appreciate it, just because.
- Be courteous to other people even if you don't know them.
- Slow down when you drive.
- Plan your car's oil changes in advance.
- When your gas tank says you are close to running out of gas, it doesn't mean you can drive another 50 miles.
- Never be late for meetings.
- Take your shoes off and put them in the same place.
- Don't be afraid to take chances and try new things.
- Teach your guy to always put down the toilet seat.
- When joking around, it's funnier if you make fun of yourself instead of someone else.

CHAPTER 35:
At the Ocean

"Why do we love the sea? It is because it has some potent power to make us think things we like to think."

– Robert Henri

Dear Lydia:

One of our family traditions, which has unintentionally developed and evolved over recent years, has been going on family vacations to Myrtle Beach, South Carolina. We call it "going to the ocean." What began when your mom and Aunt Alli were little girls who built sand castles on the beach has become a most looked forward to yearly event in our family, which has expanded to include your dad, Uncle Patrick Klein, and, for the first time in 2017, a barely walking toddler named Lydia Alleman. I watched your expression when you first laid eyes on the ocean, attempting to take in its immensity, listening to the gentle afternoon waves come into the shore, and then seeing the variety of people going into the ocean and sunbathing near the shore's edge. The expression on your face showed a creased brow as I held you and whispered "ocean" several times in your ear as you studied the vast expanse. I felt joy as I watched you make the sound *whoosh* to imitate the sound of the waves while you pointed. I thought, "Welcome to the ocean, Lydia Jeanne Alleman."

Going to the ocean has come to signify different things to different people in our family, and it can take some planning to meet the needs and wants of everyone. At the same time, those needs and wants have changed over the years. For me, going to the ocean, usually early in the summer months, symbolizes a letting go of the recently completed school year and a recharging of my internal battery. The ocean has become a tipping point for me where I can look back as well as look ahead. My advice to you is to find that place for yourself. It's so important to have a special place to keep yourself from burning out, whether it be from school or sports, during your teen years or from your career for the following forty or fifty years. Have a place where you can just sit and think.

The ocean is like a reset button. While there, I try to ask myself, "How am I different than I was last year when I came here? Have I made a difference?" The older I get, the more I think that life is really about making a difference in the lives of others. That is what I think about when I am at the ocean. I also like to reflect on where I am in my life. Life is a precious thing, and I am especially thankful for the many blessings I have received, most importantly my family. I recall your Great-Grandma Lydia explaining the "pay it forward" concept to me many years ago, and it is at Myrtle Beach that I try to put it into action the most. Not only do I try to save money throughout the year so I can pay for most things for the group there (I do refer to it as the Tank all-inclusive vacation), I understand that everyone in the family has something they enjoy the most about being there, and I want to make sure that they each get what they want. For instance, I think your Aunt Alli, who loves shopping more than anyone, somehow developed the tradition of going to the outdoor mall area there called "Broadway at the Beach." While there, she discovered a jewelry store with beautiful necklaces, and I bought one for her, your mom, and Grandma Becky. For a few years after that, we returned to the store, and more necklaces were purchased. It became one of your aunt's favorite things about her vacation. Imagine her extreme disappointment when on our 2017 vacation the store was no longer at Broadway at the Beach. I guess there will be other traditions.

In many ways, I am a people person. I like meeting new people. In 2017, your first year at the ocean, you made it seem easy. You had just learned to walk, and as only a one-year-old could do, you loved walking up to people, waving, and saying, "Hi." Many people exclaimed how cute you were. I couldn't disagree. Over the years at Myrtle Beach, I have met people from many walks of life and various parts of the United States. Nearly all have been from the South, and they were invariably friendly people who were on family vacations. When I told many of them about my first book, *Coaching Our Sons*, they often said that it sounded interesting and would like to read it. I even sent copies to a few people. I regret not having stayed in contact with them. I truly enjoyed making new friends at the ocean, and I wish them well.

When you go to the ocean, you will be expected to learn the proper beach and resort etiquette quickly. There are some things you should never do or you should always do whenever you're at the beach or the resort. The first rule involves where you place either your towel, beach chair, or umbrella if you have one (although it costs $25 a day, I choose to rent one). That area then becomes your "zone," and by midday every day as the tide comes in and the beach becomes crowded, you try not to impede anyone else's zone. If you bring your own umbrella, you may not place it in front of the rentals, blocking their views of the water. The second rule of the beach is never to throw sand. Parents teach this to their young kids almost immediately upon arrival. On a related note, often by the end of the day, it becomes windy at the beach. When you shake the sand from your towel, be aware of people sitting nearby.

Some people prefer to lounge around the various pools at the resort. Resort etiquette says that you are not allowed to place towels on chairs to save prime seats. Annoyingly, this rule is not followed by many people. The chairs remain empty all day with towels on them so that people can use the chair of their choice for a short time when they return from the beach in the late afternoon.

One thing I enjoy the most every time I go to the ocean is how the ocean hits me the first time I see it. I've come to expect it. It grabs me by the front of my shirt, looks me in the eye, and says to me, "Where have you been for so long? I've been waiting for you. You belong here." When you live in Wisconsin, seeing the ocean is a rare treat. My advice to you is to treat every visit to the ocean like it's the last time you will ever see it. You never know, it may be. The night before we would leave Myrtle Beach (when we drove back to Wisconsin, we left early in the morning), we would go down to the ocean's edge to say goodbye to the ocean. It was always a sad occasion. I always feel different when I leave. Most often I am reenergized.

To me, going to the ocean has come to reflect the ongoing circle of life, especially now that you, Lydia, are included in it. After watching my children grow up there, I now see you playing in the sand, and that thrills me. As I approach the sunset years of my life, I think it might not be a bad idea to have my ashes scattered there after I'm gone.

Lydia, one last piece of advice: Use lots of sunscreen!

CHAPTER 36:
Midwestern Values

"Optimism is the sunshine of the soul."

– Old saying

Dear Lydia:

You were born in Dodgeville, Wisconsin. Your Grandma Becky's roots are from Stevens Point, Wisconsin, by way of Minneapolis, Minnesota. Your dad's family hails from Granville, Illinois, and my family comes from the Sheboygan, Wisconsin, area. You are midwestern to your core. To some people, that is significant. It might mean that you believe certain things, have a particular set of values, and probably act a certain way. I am not saying that all of that is true for you. These traits appear to be more common in people from the Midwest. You may look at them and say to yourself, "that is not me at all." Then again, maybe it is.

People from the Midwest tend to have a strong work ethic. As your Great-Grandpa Bill Tank used to say, "Never be afraid of hard work." When you are raised in a strong blue-collar family like I was, that work ethic runs deep. It is a core value. I'm not sure, but it might have something to do with the severity of midwestern winters. In Wisconsin, the winter darkness and cold can seem unrelenting, yet, you go about your daily routine. Before I got my driver's license, I often walked four miles home after high school basketball practice in the bitter cold wintry night. I don't even remember complaining about it. I do remember that it was cold and dark as I walked along a busy highway. There were times when I got a ride from a friend or took the school's late bus, although if I did that, I was on it for an hour before being the last one dropped off.

I also think that grit is a strong midwestern value. Grit is an attitude of tenacity. It becomes that "never give up" and "refuse to lose" attitude. The most revered Wisconsin sports icons—Henry Aaron of the Milwaukee Braves, Robin Yount of the Milwaukee Brewers, and Vince Lombardi of the Green Bay Packers all had it—and their names will live forever in Wisconsin sports lore. I was raised to believe that grit could always beat a team that relied on "glitz and glitter" anytime. Of course, the national media tends to favor the opposite. Former University of Wisconsin Basketball Coach Ryan established tremendous success there and took the Badgers to the top by using a formula based on grit. Some national sports pundits criticized Wisconsin's style of play, but the Badgers always seemed to get the job done. True basketball fans understood and appreciated Coach Ryan.

A second midwestern value is problem-solving, the ability to find a solution to a problem through perseverance. While not everyone is fortunate enough to possess this ability, and I may be biased, it seems to me that many people here possess this quality. It is difficult to put a handle on what this means except that people with problem-solving skills have an inner strength they rely on during tough times which enables them to rise above adversity.

I believe that the vast majority of people in the Midwest are humble, although the media today may make it seem otherwise. While they may demonstrate great joy in victory, they don't brag about it. I cringe a little bit every time I watch a football game and see a player doing a "touchdown dance," or I watch Aaron Rodgers of the Green Bay Packers do his "championship belt demonstration." People in the Midwest like their sports heroes to be humble. They cherish Vince Lombardi's famous quote to his players, "There are three things important to every man in this locker room. His God, his family, and the Green Bay Packers. In that order." Generations have been raised on those powerful words.

Another midwestern value is the ability to care passionately about other people while helping them to become self-sufficient. That is a major source of disagreement in today's political realm. Do you take the Christian attitude that says you should always take the blessings you have been given and help people in need without question? Or do you take the Darwinian approach that stresses "survival of the fittest" and "only the strong survive"? Some people attempt to blend the two philosophies. Although I have heard the criticism, your Grandma Becky and I belive that if someone is in need, you help them. You don't even think about it.

While I want to believe that the strength of the family bond is a basic midwestern value, I am not so sure. As you know by now, family is important to me. If I was at all capable, there is nothing I would not do to help my family members through a time of need. In the same manner, I am sure that my brother would help me if I asked him. It is what we do. However, recently I have listened to several friends relate stories of family dysfunction including estrangement in which long-standing grudges are held against relatives for reasons often either long forgotten or distorted. My hope, Lydia, is that as you go down the winding path of your life, you can steer clear of these issues as I have in my family. They cause hurtful feelings, which are not easily healed. The saying, "Blood runs thicker than water," is so true. If you are fortunate enough to have younger brothers or sisters or even cousins, you will find that in our family, we stick up for each other. The family bond is a strong part of who we are.

In the Midwest, there is a guarded sense of optimism. No one likes a pessimist. When I walk the five blocks or so to Dodgeville High School at 6:15 a.m. every morning, most often I feel pretty good. I have a great passion for teaching history and helping kids in any way I can. I want to make a difference, and over the first thirty-eight years, I believe I have. That's the optimism I carry when I walk into the building. I believe that others in the Midwest share that optimism. Lydia, as you go through life, if you want people to think you're an optimist, always greet them with a smile!

CHAPTER 37:
Schmoozers

"Never be bullied into silence. Never allow yourself to be made a victim. Accept no one's definition of your life; define yourself."

– Harvey Fierstein

Dear Lydia:

No one wants to be labeled a schmoozer. A schmoozer gets what they want by schmoozing, associating with the people who can help them telling them exactly what they want to hear. Everyone else knows who the schmoozers are and who is being schmoozed. They are very friendly to those from whom they may need a favor. They will go out of their way to greet you warmly, and if you are higher up on their "schmoozing list" than another person they may be with, they will quickly ignore that other person to schmooze you. You may catch yourself at some point wondering, "Why did that just happen?" This chapter is merely meant to explain this.

When I was a successful high school basketball coach winning championships and guiding teams to state tournaments, I was schmoozed a lot by various people. It began when I became a varsity coach in my twenties in Nebraska. The program had seen some success but had struggled to win games consistently. Luckily for me, when I was elevated from junior varsity coach to head coach, I had players who loved the game intensely and played the game whenever they could, just like I did when I was young. I was the head coach there for three years with a record of 60 and 6. Parents and community members schmoozed me. I didn't understand it. My head swelled as I thought I was the one responsible for all the success and was this great coach. Remember that midwestern value of being humble? Well, I sure wasn't, although I remember telling your Grandma Becky that it won't always be like this.

Remember my advice not to get too high when you win or too down when you lose? That is especially true when you're being schmoozed. One thing that helped me keep things in perspective was the fact that I kept a file of letters I received over the years. Many of them were from very kind community people, parents, and friends expressing their thanks for what they thought I had either done for their son or for the community of Dodgeville. They were heartfelt, and I appreciated them. They were not what I called schmoozing at all. On the other hand, about once a year I would receive an anonymous letter in the mail telling me how awful of a coach I was. Some would cite recent game situations or wonder why I didn't play a certain player more (even though it was written anonymously, it was obvious who wrote the letter). Getting those negative letters made me understand the importance of developing a thick skin when you coach. On one occasion, I received letters on back-to-back days. Before reading them, my thought was, "Man, when it rains, it pours." The first letter, however, was a positive one, and the parents ended it by thanking me for having a positive impact on their son's self-esteem. The second letter, written anonymously, bashed me pretty good and said that I was a negative influence on the self-esteem of the players. Some people advised me to throw away anonymous letters, but I saved them all in a file. Whenever I was being schmoozed a lot, I got those negative letters out to burst my bubble.

It often feels good to be schmoozed. The perception is that people like you. To me, though, schmoozers are fake. They're not real with you, and they expect something in return for the schmoozing. After coaching two separate Dodgeville teams to WIAA state tournaments in the 1990s and just missing a third, I recall being at a Christmas gathering of many Dodgeville area people, prime schmoozing territory. People were socializing in a friendly way. Often, I don't enjoy these occasions because I'm not a schmoozer, and I don't like being schmoozed. When I was coaching basketball, I rarely went out socially because I didn't want to be asked why I played one player over another ten years before. In this case, however, I was talking to a few friends when a woman I didn't know came up and joined the conversation. (I found out later that she had a son who played basketball and was about to enter high school.) She smiled and flirted. I was wearing jeans and a sport coat. Before I knew it, she had slipped her hand inside the coat and briefly kept it there. I was like, "Whoa!" I knew immediately that she was a schmoozer. Two years later her son decided to no longer play basketball. When I saw the boy's mother grocery shopping, she looked the other way, acting like she didn't know me.

Kids learn the art of schmoozing quickly. They learn which parent to ask when there is something they especially want. In school, if they smile at the teacher and give them compliments, and especially if the teacher is not aware that they are being schmoozed, they are likely to receive special favors from that teacher. Students in high school see coaches schmoozing them. If a student is not a particularly good athlete or plays a different sport, a coach does not schmooze them, especially if the student was schmoozed but rejected the coach by choosing another sport. By their high school years, kids have a good understanding of the difference between a schmoozer and someone who cares about them, and that reputation travels quickly between students.

Lydia, my advice to you is don't be a schmoozer. Make your dreams come true through all the other virtues you possess, beginning with a strong work ethic. Schmoozing is a shortcut to get what you want. It feels good to be schmoozed. Now that my coaching career is finished, I am no longer schmoozed. I don't miss it at all. It is clear to me, however, the difference between those overly friendly people who were truly being good people and the ones who just wanted to capitalize on my position.

Politicians are the kings and queens of the schmoozers. They have to schmooze in order to survive. As they walk in parades and hold their news conferences, they smile and tell everyone what they want to hear. They schmooze their constituents. It's how they hope to either get elected or remain in office. Recently, I have said that the first politician running for public office who does what they say they will do, helps the people who most need it, and says nothing negative about their opponent, will get my vote. Good luck waiting for that, right?

CHAPTER 38:
Being the Rock

"Work on yourself first, take responsibility for your own progress."

– I Ching

Dear Lydia:

Being the rock means that you are steady during any crisis. Unexpected things don't rattle you. You exude a calmness that says to others that "It will be okay." When things look especially bleak, others turn to you for advice on how to handle the stress or adversity. Rocks are never schmoozers. Instead, they are solid and steady people who can be counted on to be there whenever or wherever necessary. Most people have someone they can count on to be there for them. If you don't have that person, perhaps it hasn't yet been necessary in your life. Nothing seemingly disastrous has happened yet, which is a good thing. Be prepared, though, because you never know when something unexpected can happen.

As the 2015–2016 school year was just getting started, your Grandma Becky was training to run in her eighteenth 26.2-mile marathon. It was a particularly hot end of August that year, and she was happy that her training was nearly completed. Because of the heat, she did much of her running early in the morning before work. On the Friday before Labor Day weekend, I went to school early (luckily I drove to school that day). Shortly before 7 a.m. the phone in my classroom rang like it often did at that time when either your mom or Aunt Alli would call me. This time, however, the call was from a woman who had been walking around the Dodgeville High School track. She frantically exclaimed that your Grandma Becky had fallen on the track and was badly injured. I bolted there immediately.

Grandma Becky had stumbled and fallen onto the track. Her left elbow had dislocated, her arm was broken in two places, and the bone had penetrated the skin. It was a gruesome injury. One of the things she said between screams as the EMTs were attempting to immobilize the arm was, "I'm sorry I'm such a baby!" None of us thought she was. She was taken from Upland Hills Health here in Dodgeville to the University of Wisconsin Hospital's Trauma Center where eventually two surgeries were performed. She was disappointed that she was unable to run in the marathon. She was strong throughout the hours of agonizingly painful physical therapy. She was determined to regain the range of motion and strength in her left arm. It took months, and for a time there was even the threat of having to go back into the arm and perform yet another surgery, which no one wanted. Grandma Becky showed great strength and was a rock throughout the entire process from start to finish.

Your mom is a rock. When under pressure, she doesn't get rattled. Throughout her accomplished career as a collegiate runner, she faced the pressures of high expectations, yet she never faltered and was named the UW-Platteville Female Athlete of the Year three consecutive times. Now, as a physical education teacher at Dodgeville Elementary School, she is assigned large workloads of students, classes, and extra duties, which she performs at a high level. When she leaves school at the end of the day, she is exhausted, yet she does so without complaint. She is never rattled, and a crisis only makes her stronger. The closest your mom ever came to panicking was when Grandma Becky suffered her arm accident. When she was told that there was an urgent message for her, her immediate thought was that your dad, who at that time commuted to work in Lancaster, had had a car accident. Quickly, I could let her know that was not the case. As I said, she is a rock.

So how do you know if you are a rock or not? First, you cannot be a rock if the people around you don't feel comfortable with you leading them through a time of crisis. If they perceive you to be just as rattled as they are, or if they feel like you are fake in any way, then they will shun you during the time of trial. There are no fake rocks. Second, it takes time to develop rock tendencies. Early in my coaching career, I felt like my players' confidence in my coaching abilities was there but might have been less deserved. By the last years of my career, I felt like I had earned the position as their rock, and they could rely on me.

CHAPTER 39:
Regrets

"Lost time is never found again."

– Benjamin Franklin

Dear Lydia:

As I said earlier, life goes by incredibly fast. You are now more than a year old. While most of your life still awaits you, before you know it you will be a grandparent like I am. The chapters of advice you have read so far are meant to help you through different issues and periods of your life. Maybe you will choose to ignore them. If even one piece of advice helps you, then this book is worthwhile to me. However, I hope that you can reach your later years with only a minimum number of regrets in your life. So, take these chapters of advice and give them each some thought. Not everyone receives good advice, so they must meander their way through life without it.

Because I am not a second-guesser, I don't regret many things in my life. I try to give good thought to my most important decisions in life, make them, and then not look back afterward. My first piece of advice to you here is not to be a second-guesser. Make your decision and then live with it. Some people are unable to do that. They live their entire lives in a series of second-guessed decisions, regretting even the most basic decisions. They may flip-flop the basic decisions again and again.

I have lived most of my life by following two separate paths. Unlike some athletes, who often stay away from books and academia, I have always excelled at both. When I graduated from college and became a social studies teacher in Plymouth, Wisconsin, I was asked to coach basketball. Of course I said yes, and with that, I became a teacher and a coach. I came to believe that great coaching is really great teaching. Later on, as a varsity coach, I discovered that I could transfer my automatic adrenaline on game days to my teaching in the classroom. It was still there on the day following the game. I could easily get up and teach well even though I most likely had only three or four hours of sleep the night before.

Although I went on to have a successful coaching career and have positively impacted the lives of thousands of students, I regret choosing to teach and to coach over getting my doctorate and teaching at the college level. That is probably the greatest regret that I live with today. When I share this with people, they often respond by saying that, although I am sixty-one years old and nearing the end of my career, I could still do it. It doesn't make any sense to me to spend tens of thousands of dollars on a doctorate program to teach for a few years at a college. I also briefly considered going to law school. I would have enjoyed the academic rigor and the larger salary, but I don't regret that decision. I guess I was destined to work with young people. One tremendous benefit of that decision was that it allowed me to be with my three children extensively during our summers off. Partly because of that, all three, Uncle Wes, Aunt Alli, and your mom grew up feeling loved and secure, important elements in their emotional foundation.

When I look back upon my life now, a second regret I have is that I did not figure out some of these things I am sharing with you in this book earlier. I was blind to certain things. For instance, I think I was too caught up in materialistic things. I was not empathetic enough to people who needed my help, especially students. I spent an excessive amount of time helping those students who were at the higher levels of their class and not enough time with students who felt more alienated at school. They needed my help just as much, if not more than the best and the brightest. I know that I helped them, but their success in school should have been my mission. Over recent years, I have come to understand that, and my thinking in school regarding how to connect with kids has changed radically. I regret that my internal light bulb did not go on sooner.

My advice to you, Lydia, is to stay as active throughout your life as possible. Depending on your age when you are reading this, you probably believe that you will never get old, and you will be able to run forever. I know. I've been there. I have always been athletic. I was pretty good at any sport I chose. Until I was fifty-five years old, I worked out daily by lifting weights, playing basketball, and running. In the spring of that year, I ran a trail run out at Governor Dodge State Park and felt soreness in my left ankle. There had been times in which I had felt it before, so my first thought was, "Oh well, I'm just getting old." During the following weeks when it did not get better, I went to the doctor who, after an x-ray followed by an MRI, sent me to an ankle specialist in Madison. He said it was very serious, and I should have surgery soon. Without giving it enough thought, I had the surgery and was laid up for months. Six years later, I regret that decision. I can no longer do the things I once enjoyed. It changed my life.

CHAPTER 40:
Death

"Life is a graceful soaring. Death is a graceful landing."

– Terri Guillemets

Dear Lydia:

Perhaps I should have included my advice and feelings about death to you in the "Invisible Elephants" chapter because death is something that everyone eventually thinks about but few people want to talk about. The older you get, it silently creeps into your thoughts. Suddenly, you notice that your hair keeps getting grayer, you groan when you get out of bed in the morning just like your dad used to, and you're attending more wakes or funerals for people not very far from your age. Steadily you notice that the things in your life, which were once so important, really don't mean so much anymore. You notice that the two most dominant topics of discussion with your friends have become health problems and retirement. Not to sound too morbid, but the Grim Reaper awaits everyone.

Like most people, I don't have a death wish, but I am realistic. My lineage is not good. Your mom and Aunt Alli immediately shut down the conversation whenever I tell them that throughout my family history, Tank men die young. My grandfather only lived until he was sixty-three. Great-Grandpa Bill Tank was sixty-four. Of my two brothers, Jim Tank was sixty-nine, and Jon Tank was fifty-three when they passed away. Only Mike and I survive. I understand that life is short, and life is precious. Now, am I going to break the trend and live well into my eighties somehow? I hope so. I would like nothing more than to live to see you grow up and become an adult. However, if I don't quite make it, that is the main reason why I am writing these words of advice to you and my other grandchildren. When you're thirty-five, I don't want you to be sitting at a family reunion with your Uncle Wes, Aunt Alli, Uncle Patrick, your mom, and your dad looking through old photo albums when your kids see a picture of me and wonder, "Who was this old guy?" Hopefully, these words help you and eventually your children to know me.

Although death is one of the most written about topics, and much has been said about it in religious circles, nearly all of what we know about death is speculation and conjecture. So, my beliefs and advice in this chapter may or may not be accurate. I do know for sure that even though you may not realize it now, memories do fade, but feelings and emotions do not. I see it in your face now as a one-year-old when you smile and open your arms for me to pick you up.

To me, death is just the next step in life. Unlike many people, I don't think death is the end. I believe that death here on earth is really the beginning. The afterlife is a mysterious state of being in which you are no longer contained in your physical body. However, I believe that your spirit lives on in the afterlife. You are now your spirit. When your body is buried underground or is burned in cremation, it doesn't matter because you are no longer within your body.

Many people believe that it is possible to contact and connect with their friends or loved ones in the hereafter. That does seem extreme, but I don't really know. If it is possible, I will be all for it. I don't think, though, that it is always obvious. Take for, instance, your Great-Grandmother Mary Jane Thompson, who passed away from cancer in 2001. When she was alive, she always had a special thing for birds and cardinals in particular. At one Christmas, she bought everyone in the extended family a small imitation tweeting bird because she thought they were cute. A few years after her death, when I took your Aunt Alli prom dress shopping, we searched everywhere for just the right dress for her to wear to her junior prom.

We finally found it at a store in Madison. As we went to pay for it, I told your Grandma Becky to listen because I could distinctly hear a bird chirping over the store's intercom. We both looked at each other and felt that it was her mom giving her thumbs up on the dress choice. Some would have said, and I agree that Great-Grandma Mary Jane, who was nearly 100 percent Irish-American, was a party animal. Your Aunt Alli comes by that trait quite honestly. On many different occasions and in a variety of places, when we have held family gatherings, suddenly a cardinal will appear. We just believe that your great-grandmother refuses to be excluded from the party.

Anyway, I don't fear death, and my advice is that you should not fear it either. It is also just as important that you don't ignore death either. Talk about it! It's going to happen to all of us someday, hopefully later rather than sooner. When I die, try not to be too sad, and try not to cry too much. I have lived a great life for which I am very thankful. Celebrate my life! If you're old enough, or if your mom and dad allow it, give a toast and drink a beer on my behalf! One thing I do want you to think about, though, is that I loved you more than anything, and you brought great joy into my life. As Abraham Lincoln's Secretary of War said at the president's deathbed, "Now he belongs to the ages."

Funerals and wakes are for the living. Like most people, I do not enjoy going to them, but I go out of respect for those who are no longer with us and to extend my condolences to family members. Lavish funerals are not necessary to impress anyone. In recent years, I have changed my mind. I think I would rather be cremated. For a while, I liked the idea of a cemetery resting site with a gravestone with my name on it and Grandma Becky later buried next to me. I like the fact that I can see my parents' gravesites in the Sheboygan Falls Cemetery whenever I can make a trip to my hometown. It gives me comfort. But now I am not so sure. I don't get creeped out by the fact that my body is going to be in a coffin buried under six feet of earth. As I said earlier, the body is no longer who I am. I am now my spirit.

I am also not that big on funeral homes either. I would really like to have a gathering at my house, and, if it's a nice day (one of a handful we get in Wisconsin every year), sit out on the basketball court, drink beer, and tell stories. Have a celebration of life!

Please note, I am not finished yet. Everyone makes a difference and then leaves their legacy. I often wonder what legacy am I leaving behind. I often look with pride at your Uncle Wes, Aunt Alli, your mom and you, and I think, "There is my legacy." If my mom and dad are looking down and waiting for me to join them, I will be anxious to talk to them and share the joy I feel in my heart for you.

PART 3: Relationships

CHAPTER 41:
The Family Foundation

"Other things may change us, but we start and end with family."

– Anthony Brandt

Dear Lydia:

Your family is where your life begins. As a baby, you know immediately if you are loved or not. Your mom, dad, and grandparents are going to be there to support you in any way possible. You were born into a family with an especially strong emotional foundation. Throughout the first year of your life, you have found that your mom and dad are always there to meet your daily needs. When you are hungry, you are fed. When you need to have your diaper changed, it is changed. When you are tired, you are put in your crib (even if you fight it because you don't want to miss anything!). You also receive a great deal of affection from just about everyone, signified by the fact that you smile and say, "Hi" to anyone within eyesight. These things combined create your strong family foundation.

Over my many years as a high school history teacher, I have seen thousands of teenage boys and girls come and go in my classroom. Some students are very successful in my class, while I must get creative to find the best way for other students to learn. I believe that all students want to learn if I can find the most effective way for them to do so. It isn't always easy. I haven't always taught with this overriding philosophy. At one time, I am sorry to say, I believed in "one size fits all." In other words, if the student did not do exactly what was required and they didn't earn the number of points required, then it wasn't my fault if they failed. They chose to fail. I was also offered various strategies to help kids who were struggling to learn.

Years into my career, I finally realized that my thinking was wrong. Having had my own three children go through high school helped me come to this realization. The first thing I discovered was that everyone has strengths, and everyone has weaknesses. With my three kids as well as with others who, I believe, had come from strong family backgrounds, I did not think they were any smarter than any of their peers. The greatest difference for them was that they went to school every day with that strong family foundation.

At the beginning of every school year, your Grandma Becky and I would sit down at the kitchen table with your mom and Aunt Alli and discuss the upcoming school year. I told them that classes and sports seasons could have their ups and downs. They might not like a certain class or teacher. They might have disagreements with each other or with friends, but no matter what, we would always be there for them. We had their backs. That strong family foundation carried over into their college years and now their adult years.

When you have a solid family foundation on which to fall back, it allows you to go out into the world to seek your fortune while at the same looking over your shoulder for support. Someday you are going to feel a great sense of gratitude to your mom and dad like I do for giving this to you. Someday you too will most likely be a grandmother and pass along some of the advice which I have shared with you in this book. Someday, you are going to look back at your own life and ponder, "I wonder what my Grandfather Chuck Tank would think of that?" I don't know the answer to that one, but I do know every time you end a phone call or leave someone by saying, "I love you," as we do in our family, you are strengthening your family bond. As I said earlier, if you take care of the little things, the big things take care of themselves.

So, how important is your family? Some families break up when some members become estranged and don't speak to each other. Other people choose material things over their families. My advice to you is to be wary of that and be upfront about your family when you start getting serious with a guy.

Remember that when you marry a guy, you are really marrying his family. As I told you earlier about the Irish, family is everything. At any family gathering, you will be the first one there and the last one to leave. Communicating is critical. Talking is always good (even when he doesn't want to!). That is how you will eventually get to know him as well as his family.

CHAPTER 42:
Family Traditions

"A wise woman once said to me that there are only two lasting bequests we can hope to give our children. One of these she said is roots, the other, wings."

– William Hodding Carter

Dear Lydia:

Every family has rituals and traditions, which are constantly performed over time. Family members may or may not be aware of them, and later they may not even understand why they perform them, but everyone in the family understands their roles within the rituals and traditions. Gradually the family may assume that they are simply something everyone does. These traditions probably lend a sense of comfort and security to their lives. They are what you do every day. For instance, everyone sits at a designated place at the dinner table with your father sitting at the head of the table. Or when your family drives somewhere he automatically drives. When he's gone, everything else seems a little bit off. My advice to you is to thoughtfully look at your family's traditions because they help you see your true identity.

Most family traditions, no matter how obscure or inconsequential they may seem, are rarely questioned. They are what I call "givens." It is a "given" that a certain tradition is honored by everyone in the family. If an outsider questions why something is done, they are probably greeted with a shocked blank stare, which says to the person, "No one has ever questioned this before. How dare you?" For instance, Grandma Becky's family roots are in the Minneapolis, Minnesota, area. When our family goes there to attend weddings, funerals, or family reunions, it has become a family tradition that we have to stop somewhere and eat chow mein. When I questioned that tradition, I was greeted with a death stare, which in effect told me, "What were you thinking? This is the greatest chow mein ever. They don't make it like this anywhere else." Lesson learned.

When I think of my family's traditions, one stands out above all the rest. My mother's father, Gottlieb Seidenzahl, as family lore has it, started it. My parents, Bill and Lydia Tank, continued it with my brother's children when they were young. Unfortunately, they passed away before my three children were born. I have been waiting a long time to continue the tradition with you, and just this spring, when you turned one, I did it. The tradition is to create and designate a "special spot" just for you. Every time you come over to Grandma and Grandpa Tank's house, there is a secret surprise waiting for you in your spot. It might be a book, a toy, or a box of animal crackers, your current favorite, but whatever it is, you know that it's just for you. When you arrive at our house, you immediately go to your "special spot." It's a family tradition that helps strengthen our bond because each grandchild is made to feel special.

Recently, I have tried to initiate a new tradition. I bought you a special box for your first birthday. I wrote a letter to you on your first birthday and put it in the box. That box and that letter are yours to keep, and I intend to write you a birthday letter on your birthday every year for the rest of my life. Family traditions are supposed to mean something. How do I know this will mean something to you? I try to ask myself if this is something I would treasure had my grandparents done this for me seventy or eighty years ago. When I say, "Absolutely," then I know I have hit a home run. Lydia, my advice to you is to write birthday letters to your grandchildren when they are born and get older. Hopefully, they will cherish them.

When I was a young boy in the early 1960s, before thousands of miles of interstate highways traversed the United States, family vacations were, for the most part, confined to lake cottages in Wisconsin or visiting relatives in neighboring states. During the early 1980s and early in our marriage, your Grandma Becky and I took a few trips to historic sites in the East and West. During the five years we lived in Nebraska in the late 1980s, it seemed like our family vacations revolved around traveling back to Wisconsin to visit relatives, and as a young family in the early 1990s, we were just trying to keep our heads above water financially.

During the late 1990s, however, when our children were young, our family had unintentionally established a new tradition, which has grown over the years. Almost by accident, we first went to Myrtle Beach, South Carolina, as your Uncle Wes was about to enter high school. We did not realize it at the time, and it took years for me to understand, but the ocean always seemed like the right fit for us. We went to other very nice places, but for us they never quite seemed to measure up to the ocean at Myrtle Beach. I can see this becoming a family tradition for following generations.

Some family traditions are small, and you might be unaware that they are even traditions. They are simply things you do without thinking. My advice to you is to think about why you are doing something. Don't just do something because you have always done it that way. On the other hand, if it works for you, then fine. An example of that is Christmas Eve. When I was a boy, our family always attended the Christmas Eve service at St. Paul's Lutheran Church in Sheboygan Falls. The candlelight singing of "Silent Night" still brings tears to my eyes as I remember my family. It was a very spiritual moment. Following that, our family went home and opened Christmas gifts. (I could never understand why some people opened their presents in the morning). The tradition has remained with my family now decades later. To me, Christmas wouldn't seem right without it, and I think my kids feel the same way.

As I told you earlier, memories tend to fade away. Family traditions, however, keep those thoughts and feelings alive in your mind. As you know, I grew up in a strong German-American household dominated by males with my mother's influence. Germans love to eat, and a strong German family tradition is to provide a lot of food at all gatherings. German potato salad, baked beans, and bratwurst on a Sheboygan hard roll, as well as many incredibly delicious desserts, were staples when all of my mother's siblings' families gathered on a Sunday afternoon. No one ever left hungry. If I could go back nearly sixty years to those Sunday gatherings for even thirty minutes, I would do it in a second. Today, when my kids come home, there is always lots of food.

Sometimes, no matter how hard you try, family traditions die out. As adults, cousins no longer stay in touch. Their parents wish they would, but the connections just aren't there. As the grandson of German immigrants who only spoke German within their household, I grew up hearing many German words. My parents spoke the language fluently. Although I took two years of the subject in high school, I have lost much of it. Occasionally, I recall certain German words. Some stand out (please forgive me if I misspell them). The meanings are mine:

- **Schlecht:** If a little kid knows that they are getting away with something, they are referred to as schlecht. Lydia, as I have watched you develop over the last year, many times I have said that you have given me a look that says you are schlecht. I can almost sense your Great-Grandmother Lydia looking down and whispering it in my ear.

- **Punshka:** Also known as a Punsh, this might be a Polish reference from Stevens Point where your Grandma Becky grew up. I believe that a punshka is a reference to a prune-filled donut. Your Aunt Alli has referred to you affectionately as a punshka whenever she sees you.

- **Babushka:** This is a scarf that covers your head. Perhaps this comes from the Volga River Germans, many of whom emigrated to the United States at the turn of the twentieth century from Russia. I recall my mother covering our heads for a short time with a thin scarf saying, "My little babushka!"

- **Schwap:** I'm not sure why, but a common thing to do was to cup your hand and slap the back of your thigh, creating a *schwap* sound. A lot of us did it, but I cannot remember why.

There are probably many other old German words that I grew up with but cannot remember.

CHAPTER 43:
Red Flags, Green Flags

"Love many, trust few, always paddle your own canoe."

– Author unknown

Dear Lydia:

No one is perfect. When you begin dating guys (the longer you wait to date, the better!), hormones begin racing through your body and will cloud your brain. If he is a guy you are attracted to, you may not even be able to think. You may be fourteen years old and believe that you, without any doubt in your mind, have discovered the guy of your dreams. You believe that he is "the one." I knew one girl who had dated a friend of mine beginning in eighth grade, through their high school years, and all through their college years. Upon graduation, she broke up with him and promptly married another guy.

In this section on relationships, I want to talk about red flags and green flags. These are the behaviors and personality traits that other people around you are seeing in the guy you're dating, while your brain is cloudy and unable to see the truth. One red flag might be a small issue that isn't troubling and is easy to overlook. However, if you see ten small red flags, then that becomes a major issue. Early in your relationship, consider the question, "How many red flags become a deal breaker?" On the other hand, just one red flag might be a deal breaker, impossible to overlook. Green flags could also be big or small, depending on your priorities. Large green flags are the great qualities in the guy you're dating and are often the reason why people overlook red flags or even deal breakers.

Of course, there needs to be a fair amount of compromise in every relationship. I call this the 70–30 rule. This means that, unlike the myth that long-lasting relationships should always be 50–50, relationships are continually swinging back and forth somewhere in the 70–30 range. There are times when you will give in 70 percent of the time, and times when he will do the same. There are people with extreme personalities who demand that the other person give in all the time. Of course, to most people that is a deal breaker. On the other hand, if a guy is willing to remain beside you at the 100–0 level during extended periods of major stress in your life such as a health problem, that is a major green flag. The problem is that you may not find this out until you are committed to that person or married to him.

Red flags sometimes appear when you least expect them. I think the first potential red flag or green flag is how a guy treats other people. He may feel justified to go into a rage at the least provocation by someone. Eventually, he will do the same to you. Also, how a guy treats his mother is a great indicator early in your relationship of how he will treat you after the two of you are married. Related to that, if you take my earlier advice and go out of your way to be nice to another person, and he cannot comprehend why you would hold a door open for someone or stop your car and wait for someone to walk slowly across a crosswalk, that is a red flag. Also, never enter a relationship with a guy thinking that he will change or that you have some magical ability to change him because he loves you. It's not about love. It's about who he is and how he was raised. No matter what, in his mind he is right.

Control is a big red flag in any relationship. I see it in high school relationships every year. Anytime a guy tries to pressure you into doing things you're not comfortable doing, that is a red flag. For instance, if a guy wants to begin a sexual relationship, and you are not ready, you should never do it simply to please him. In a healthy relationship where he truly cares about you as much as he says he does, the guy would be fine with that. He would never want anything from you that you were not comfortable giving him. On a similar note, I have always thought that ultimatums are never good, although if you give someone an ultimatum, you better be prepared to stand behind what you said if he chooses something you don't want. But if a guy gives you an ultimatum such as, "Have sex with me or I am leaving," my advice is to run from him as fast as you can. (Again, I have a feeling you are going to be a fast runner!). Remember that ultimatums and control say more about the person talking than they do about the actual situation.

So, what are a few other red flags you should be on the lookout for in a relationship? If a guy thinks very highly of himself, drop him quickly. Similarly, run from a guy who is a known player because he always will be (even if he is good-looking). Even on the first date, if he spends most of the time talking about himself and his accomplishments, or later he wants to impress you with his money, that is a deal breaker. On the other hand, does he spend time getting to know you by listening to you and caring about your beliefs, thoughts, and opinions? If he does, that is a big green flag. Always remember that if he doesn't listen to you, he really doesn't care about what you have to say.

A large difference in age can be a red flag, but it doesn't necessarily have to be. I think that socioeconomic difference is a greater red flag. If a guy comes from a background of far greater or lesser wealth than you do, he was probably raised differently than you were. This can cause problems. The older you get, the age difference becomes less important. In most cases, however, I think that if a guy is much older than you are, that is a red flag. On a side note, if he is quite a bit older and divorced, being divorced is not a red flag if he is willing to talk about what happened and why. If he refuses to accept any blame or blames his ex for all their problems, that is a red flag. When I was a guest speaker in a senior level class doing a unit on relationships, a common question was, "What is a good age to get married?" My response was that there is none. More importantly, "How well do you know yourself?" and "How well do you know him?"

My last piece of advice here is to listen carefully to what your parents or other mentors have to say. They will give you great insight on potential boyfriends. If a guy ever comes between you and your parents, or if he wants you to keep secrets from your parents, that too is a red flag. The two big questions, though, you are going to come to grips with are, "What do you consider deal breakers in a relationship?" and "How many red flags equal a deal breaker?" If you can answer those questions, you will be way ahead of most people in the relationship game, and it's possible that you may save yourself from a lot of heartache later.

CHAPTER 44:
Love and Looks

"Love is the irresistible desire to be irresistibly desired."

– Robert Frost

Dear Lydia:

When babies are born, they arrive in the world with a genetic predisposition to look a certain way. To their parents and grandparents, all babies look cute. To outsiders, the small physical imperfections are a little more apparent. When you were born and throughout your first year, I was blind to anything but the fact that you were the cutest baby ever born. Of course, it didn't help that you were born with big cheeks and chubby, baby fat arms and thighs. Everyone said how cute you were. As you entered your toddler stage and would flash your beautiful smile, wave, and say, "Hi" to strangers, nearly all would smile back and say how cute you were. I was briefly concerned that you were going to grow up hearing that and would put too much emphasis on your looks.

Some people base their entire lives on how they look. They spend countless hours either exercising in the gym, at home or outside. While it promotes overall good health, their primary reason might be to lose weight in order to look better. The media today bombards everyone with what is supposed to look good. On television, in movies, and magazines, beautiful young people place subtle pressure on teens hundreds of times every day. No wonder girls of normal weight at times complain of being overweight. Eating disorders can develop in an attempt to lose weight.

Lydia, don't misunderstand me, everyone likes to look good. As you get older, you will start to notice how guys look, and it will give you a little thrill when you discover that guys are checking you out. It's a ritual. My advice to you, however, is that while good looks are important, and you should want to look your best, they are not *that* important. Your mom is someone who appears to have this pretty much well in hand. I recall a time when your mom was in eighth grade preparing for high school. Along with Aunt Alli and Grandma Becky, the four of us went on a training run at Governor Dodge State Park. While on the run, the topic of what clothes girls should wear to school came up. Your mom simply stated that she hadn't given it much thought, but her typical school uniform of choice was to throw on a pair of running shoes, comfortable sweatpants, and a sports t-shirt. Aunt Alli rolled her eyes, aghast, and stated, "You have got to be kidding!" as if this wardrobe snafu was some poor reflection on her. Your mom and her older sister are both beautiful young women, but it was Alli who taught your mom about style.

Children learn at a very early age about the importance of beauty and appearance. Any advice I give you is not going to change that. In today's world, girls can be vicious toward other girls because of how they look, especially if they see them as territorial rivals. Social media is alive with posts which can reduce girls to tears over the slightest appearance adjustment. It is of greatest importance to me, Lydia, that you understand that just because a girl is prettier than you are on the outside and maybe is more popular than you are in the "elite" social group, that does not mean that she is better than you are. Your Grandma Becky and I raised our three kids to understand the importance of inner beauty. Naturally, people's outer looks change over time. Some people become more good-looking, while others less so. Outer beauty will always fade, while inner beauty always shines through.

At the same time, never let a guy get away with saying something negative about how you look just because you are female. You live in a world today in which some guys think it's okay to comment on how girls, whom they don't know, look. Don't let anyone make you feel bad. We currently have a president who thinks it's okay to do that. I do not agree.

On a related but different note, what is the difference between love and infatuation? I'm not sure that I can honestly answer that one except to say that they both make you feel really good, but infatuation often does not turn out the way you thought it would. When you are infatuated with someone, your heart goes "pitter-pat," for a time, and you might not even know why you are attracted to him. Later, when the relationship is over, you probably no longer see what you saw in him.

Sometimes having a boyfriend or having the "right" boyfriend can become a matter of status. Years ago, that might have been a star athlete in the school, but I don't see that happening as much today as it once did. Personally, I think it's better to wait to have a boyfriend. You might think you're emotionally ready, but most likely you are not. Having boys as friends is a good way to be around them without the emotional drama. In high school, it's common for upperclassmen to "swoop in" on the more innocent younger girls, and you might even feel flattered by their attention. My advice, however, is to wait.

One common mistake that many people make is thinking that they can make someone fall in love with them. Of course, most people who know that think that others who attempt that are wrong, but they are the exception to the rule, and they fall into the trap. My advice to you, Lydia, is that if he "isn't that into you," let him go. The quick break is always better than the agonizingly slow breakup death. Similar to that is unrequited love when you love someone, and they don't love you back. That hurts, but again, let him go. I guarantee there will be others who will replace him.

CHAPTER 45:
Dating

"You learn to like someone when you find out what makes them laugh, but you can never truly love someone until you find out what makes them cry."

— Author unknown

Dear Lydia:

Many times, the dating relationship can be about power. Who has the greater amount of power in the relationship, and how do they use it? When a guy is considering asking a girl out, he knows that all of the power is in her hands. There are various ways that guys or girls today can ask each other out for the first time. Of course, times have changed. The first time I asked a girl out on a date, I was so nervous before I called her at her home. Unlike today, we only had one phone in our house, and it was in the kitchen, the central location of the house, with a cord. I had to wait for the opportunity in which no one else was around. I recall my rapid heartbeat and the sweaty palms as I dialed and prayed that she would answer. She did. Today, of course, there are a number of ways of getting to know someone or asking them out more easily. I could only wish that was true back in 1972.

My greatest pieces of dating advice are to be nice no matter what, don't play games by making him guess things, and just be yourself. If you can consistently stick to these three things, I believe things will work out well for you. First, being nice no matter what can take some courage, but that says the most about you as a person. Some people make the mistake of returning one mean thing for another, especially in high school relationships. If the date didn't go well, and both of you know it, don't go on social media and say anything about it. On the other hand, if he decides to tell his friends how badly it went and said bad things about you on social media, my advice is not to engage him; leave it alone.

Second, I don't believe in playing games. People who aren't mature enough to be in a solid relationship tend to be game players. They can lure you in and then cast you out over and over. If you don't want to go out with Elmer, don't say, "I'm busy," when he asks fourteen times. If you know from the beginning that he's not the right one for you, don't lead him on until you can find an acceptable backup.

And third, just be yourself. If you are fortunate enough to grow up to be anything like your mom or your dad, I have a strong feeling that you are going to grow up to be a beautiful young woman on the inside as well as the outside. When you begin to date, that will quickly become apparent to whoever is the lucky guy.

When you start going out with boys, you are probably going to hear at some point sooner rather than later that they are only interested in one thing. It's true, but it's not what you think it is. If a guy wants a girlfriend so that his friends think he's cool, that's one thing. However, never forget that what he needs most is for you to think he is the greatest. In his mind, he might be wondering why a girl as beautiful and lovely as you would be interested in a guy as dorky as him. If you make him feel good about himself, he will be yours forever.

When you begin seriously dating a guy, I suggest that you have a lengthy discussion about the differences between love and intimacy. Entire books have been written about the two of them, and I do not proclaim to be an expert on either one. The differences are subtle. What I would suggest to you is if you deeply love someone, that love will naturally evolve. If you are committed to that person, you will put your own life on the line for them if you had to. Intimacy is a deeper level of communication. The two of you have peeled away the emotional layers. People who are intimate with each other should not withhold secrets from the other. Sleeping with someone is often called "being intimate." You are removing physical layers as well as emotional layers. This always makes me wonder, "Why would a girl sleep with a boy if he was unable to communicate in other ways with her?" On a related note, never send anyone any pictures of yourself that you wouldn't be comfortable sending to your mom and dad as well. As far as sexting goes, remember that just because you delete messages, they can be recovered.

A few dating red flags:

- If a guy says to you that "He just wants to be friends with you," it's over. No matter what you do, you won't win him back. Move on.
- When a guy takes you home, he should always have you home a few minutes <u>before</u> your parents said they wanted you home.
- If a guy cares more about his friends than you.
- It is a red flag if the two of you spend more time on your phone while on the date than talking to each other.
- When you're dating during high school or college, he should always care about what your parents think.
- If a guy wears what you believe to be about a gallon of cologne, it's only because he likes you and wants to impress you.

According to your Grandma Becky, your Great-Grandma Mary Jane Thompson, who was a very strict Catholic before passing away from cancer in 2001, had one dating rule for her daughters. "Kiss a lot, but that's all." It was a good rule.

Also regarding dating, your Great-Grandfather Papa D Alleman related the following story of his first date with your Great-Grandma Jeanne. "I met Jeanne at the eighth-grade country school." At an early music concert "I played a clarinet solo, and she sang. She was a knockout. We were the same age, and she stood right in front of me at the concert. I thought she sang to me. I fell in love with her right then." Later during their freshmen year, "When we went to lunch, the girls sat on one side of the cafeteria, and the boys on the other, but I would always say, 'Hi.' During that freshman year, she started going with me. I think we were fourteen or fifteen years old. On a Friday night, I went to her house to take her to a movie. Her older sister was there visiting at the time. Her mother, who was a widow, let me in and told me to wait in the parlor. I sat and sat and sat. Finally, Jeanne came in sort of half crying and said that her sister told her mother that we were too young to date. So, I ended up going down to Bill's Snack Bar and drank Cokes all night. We went steady the next year as sophomores."

CHAPTER 46:

Getting Your Heart Broken

"Giving up doesn't always mean you are weak; sometimes it means that you are strong enough to let go."

– Author unknown

Dear Lydia:

When you're going through a heart-wrenching breakup with someone for whom you cared deeply, you probably hear one of several typical responses from friends and relatives who mean well but miss the mark. Some people will put their arms around you and try to pamper you into feeling better. They might take you shopping or eat ice cream with you all night while watching movies. Others will try to brush it off by saying things like, "It's no big deal. There are plenty of other fish in the sea." A third person or group will take your side by saying something to the effect of, "Well, he was a real jerk anyway. I didn't want to tell you this, but everybody knew he was cheating on you." No matter how much it hurts, everyone goes through this at some point, and some people get their hearts broken multiple times. It's never fun.

Everyone has their insecurities and areas of vulnerability which no one discusses, or in some cases even know exist. They might have certain elephants in the room, which we discussed in an earlier chapter. Maybe their issues are apparent such as problems with body image, or their family might live in poverty. Or perhaps their issues might be far less apparent. In effect, their issues could be buried deep within the person's psyche, and even they have a difficult time identifying the source of their feelings. (Remember, how well do you really know yourself?)

You have probably heard the phrase, "Still waters run deep." It means that there are people who aren't comfortable saying much, and though they may be quiet and shy, they still have a lot to say. They just choose to keep it inside. The ability to communicate does not come easily to them. Only those closest to them can understand. So when their feelings are hurt, that bruised emotion stays bottled up inside them. Rarely do you see significant emotional outbursts from them. (Grandma Becky, the cardiac rehab nurse, has said that because they cannot express their feelings, they are at greater risk for heart attacks later in life.) When they shed their tears, most often it's when they are alone.

Your mom is a lot like me in that way. In part, it's why I wasn't a "yeller" and a "screamer" while I was roaming the sidelines of the basketball court. I kept my emotions bottled up. When people complimented me on how composed I seemed to be while coaching during big games, I thought, "If they only knew." I understood what your mom felt when in high school she either lost a basketball game and hadn't played very well or ran what was for her a bad race. She wanted to be alone, so her mom and I gave her time to be by herself.

One of the most difficult parts of parenting is watching your child suffer any physical or emotional pain. Your mom liked one boy who was also in her class early in her high school years. He seemed like a nice boy who treated her nicely, and he seemed to be fine with the fact that I was a teacher and coach in the school. They went to movies together and liked to "hang out." He spent time at our house, and she spent time at his. Your mom felt the incredible feeling of falling in love.

At one point, however, fairly early in the relationship during the summer, your mom had been putting in a lot of training miles and playing in basketball tournaments. She became physically rundown and got sick. As her parents, we decided it would be in her best interest to make sure she recovered by getting a lot of rest, so we told her she could not go to her boyfriend's house until she was feeling significantly better. She understood and was fine with it. Her boyfriend, on the other hand, was not. It was his impression that we were too controlling. When their next date was supposed to take place a short time later, he stood her up. Your mom, who was already feeling pulled in two different directions by her boyfriend and her parents, knew very quickly that the relationship was over. The look on her face showed her utter disappointment with tears welling up in her eyes as she waited on our front porch that evening to be picked up by him, the ride that never came. Her heart had been broken.

As I stated in an earlier chapter, your mom and Aunt Alli are only sixteen months apart and have always been emotionally close to each other. They are "the girls" and are as close as any two siblings could be. While growing up, they each had their own bedroom, but for long stretches, one would move their mattress into the other's room so they could sleep together. They also shared each other's clothes. When they argued, it was with great ferocity. However, Alli was the older one of the two and was always there to protect her younger sibling. When a boy broke your mom's heart, Aunt Alli was there for her in total support. While your mom handled the breakup with grace, your Aunt Alli allowed her Irish temper to show through. While she did not confront the boy for what she perceived to be her sister's mistreatment, she let it be known that she was not happy about it at all. As always, she was there for her. Lydia, never forget that's what families are all about.

Couples break up in a variety of ways every day, and your mom's breakup, while it hurt her feelings, was not done in a mean-spirited way, and they eventually remained friends. Their romantic relationship concluded just as the social media revolution was about to explode. In the past, students were restricted to passing notes in the classroom or hallways between classes. They would have stood by lockers and talked for a few brief moments. Today, we live in an age in which many students in high schools are addicted to their screens.

Their iPhones have become their lifelines to communicating their feelings. When a relationship is crumbling, that is especially the case. In social media forums, it can often become nasty very quickly. Lydia, my advice to you is to let it go and never get into a social media war over a guy. No guy is worth that.

The deeper you get into a romantic relationship, the more vulnerable you become. That's what real intimacy is all about. You know your partner's weaknesses. When you become emotionally intimate with someone, you may feel the desire, or he may pressure you to become physically intimate as well. Be careful. Once you cross that line with him, there's no going back. If a breakup occurs after you have had sex with a guy, it will likely be much more difficult for you than for him. Remember, if a guy loves you, he won't pressure you.

CHAPTER 47:
Mean People

"He who angers you conquers you."

– Elizabeth Kenny

Dear Lydia:

It is a common belief that some people are born mean. It makes no difference whether or not they were correctly raised by parents who gave them all the opportunities to grow up to become contributing members of society. Perhaps they were seemingly raised identically to their siblings who went on to become corporate leaders who headed up foundations to help the homeless or other worthy causes. Instead, they became law-breaking criminals whose every intention was to steal from the needy. When people view the actions of the two siblings in disbelief, their response is often, "Well, I guess some people are just born mean."

Meanwhile, there are people whose environment practically assures that they will grow up to become mean. Perhaps they were raised by a physically abusive parent or a sibling who physically and emotionally tormented them. For them, every day became a struggle for survival. Without the proper counseling, children who grow up with that continue the cycle with their children. It is the saddest thing. (As teachers, we need to find a way to help those kids survive and thrive. Lydia, if you can find a way to do that in life, you will be a great success.)

I am neither a counselor nor a therapist. However, I do tend to see the good in all people. I also disagree that some people are naturally born mean. I believe that at some key point in their lives, an incident perhaps triggers something in them to become mean. When people such as career criminals, rapists, or serial killers make the national news, I always wonder what happened to them in their past to make them turn out that way. Although they are the perpetrators, I still feel sorry for them.

Over the years I have taught high school-age teenagers, I have seen and come to know some troubled young people, and I have attempted to reach out to them. Some of them have thick emotional layers guarding them. I hope that, despite their painful past, they can somehow come to see me as a person they can feel free to reach out to and perhaps even trust. I understand that it might not happen immediately. Maybe down the road, or even as adults raising their children, they will look back and remember me as someone in school who cared about them or at least as someone who gave them a fair shake. My advice to you, Lydia, is that as you walk down the path of life, remember that kindness is never a weakness. Indeed, kindness beats mean people every time.

Sometimes I believe that a person's four years in high school become magnified in their importance. (I know, I have put my high school years back in the early 1970s under the microscope for you in this book!) High school can fly by in what feels like ten minutes. You start out as a scared freshman hoping you don't get lost in the building. Then as soon as you can snap your fingers, you hear your name read aloud as you take that walk across the stage in the gym on graduation day before moving on in the world. Although your high school years are significant for laying the groundwork for your future, try not to make those years bigger than they are. Your life is in front of you and becomes what you make of it over the following sixty or seventy years.

Sadly, some students are bullied by mean people throughout their elementary, middle, and high school years. While I wish it were otherwise, I know that bullying goes on in schools every day. Bullies tend to zero in on people they perceive to be weak and exploit them in any way they can. They can make the lives of others a living hell. If you become interested in the topic of bullying in schools, I recommend that you read these two books: *Please Stop Laughing at Me* by Jodee Blanco and *Sticks and Stones: Defeating the Culture of Bullying and Rediscovering the Power of Character and Empathy* by Emily Bazelon. I have three pieces of advice to you regarding bullying during your pre-adult years. First, tell someone in a position of authority. If you are not satisfied with how the situation is handled, don't settle. (Bullies are often quite adept at turning on the charm and getting authority figures to side with them.) Simply go to someone with authority over that person. Second, no one has the right to make you feel bad and especially make you feel bad consistently. High school bullies can impact people for the rest of their lives. Don't give them that power over you. Third, if you ever see someone being bullied, don't look the other way. Be a friend to the person being picked on. It's always easier not to get involved. I hope that you step up for the person who needs it.

Some friends are fake friends. They smile and act nice to your face but talk behind your back after you are gone. My advice to you is that if you want a friend, then be a friend. As fake friends get older, they often discover that they have few true friends and probably never did throughout their lives.

CHAPTER 48:
Abuse

"The man who strikes first admits that his ideas have given out."

– Chinese proverb

Dear Lydia:

It is every father and grandfather's nightmare that their daughter or granddaughter becomes trapped in an abusive relationship. The guy she loves and has committed herself to has shown himself to have a dark side. He has hidden that side of himself well during the early part of the relationship. He knows it's there. She doesn't. He appeared to be kind and loving to her as well as the other women in his family. Perhaps there was an incident or two when he became a little too overly aggressive, but she believed that he had a kind heart and would never do anything to hurt her. Maybe she even thought that it was her fault. He's good at shifting the blame. Plus, he possessed many future husband qualities she was looking for. She had already invested so much time into the relationship. She believed that he was the "one" for her. This relationship has dysfunction written all over it. Does this sound like the plot for a bad *Lifetime* film? Of course it does, but people become involved with abusers every day.

My dad, Bill Tank, was a strong man. He was a hard worker who also had a very tender side to him. He earned extra income by boxing at the Sheboygan Armory during the Great Depression of the 1930s. It was very seldom that I saw him angry, and I could count on one hand the number of times I saw him argue with my mother. Never did he become physically violent with her. The comment that stood out the most, however, was when the topic of spouse abuse did come up, all my mother had to do to shut it down quickly was to say, "Just once." In other words, there would be no second chance. It never happened. My advice to you, Lydia, is the same. If it ever happens, there are no "do-overs."

Abuse can begin early in relationships. Although sometimes it's not easy for others to pick up on, an abusive pattern is taking shape in high school. What are some of the red flags to watch out for in abusive relationships? Again, I am not an expert, but I can share some things for you to think about. First, does he try to control you? If you are constantly having to check in with him and explain where you were or who you were with, or get permission to do things, that can be a red flag. Please note, however, that if you do some of those things on your own, that's being courteous. Along with that, if you're always worried that he is going to be angry at you, and you're "walking on eggshells" around him, then he is controlling you. If the first thing you say to him when you see him after a time apart is, "I'm sorry," then you are being controlled, and that is a form of abuse.

Abusive people cannot control themselves. They may be intelligent and become successful in other areas of their lives. A good friend of mine told me how his daughter married a doctor of medicine. Shortly into their marriage, he became abusive to her. They divorced. Some men also abuse drugs or alcohol. The combination can become lethal. They will go back and forth between abusing you and apologizing for their actions. Remember that guys who love you don't hit you. Even if he apologizes and promises with tears in his eyes that he will never do it again, do not listen to him. Get out.

Of course, it becomes more difficult to leave a relationship if there are children involved. An abuser will attempt to use the children to get you to stay with him. Know too that an abuser will at some point use the children to get back at you. He knows how important your children are to you. Don't make the mistake of thinking that he will always do what is best for his children. People in abusive relationships don't think that way. They merely want to retaliate against you for how they perceive they were wronged. He cares more about himself than he does his children. You are their mother. Protect your children. Remember, no matter what he says to the contrary, it is not your fault, and it is not the fault of your children.

Sometimes abusers don't physically abuse. Emotional abuse can be just as damaging to anyone and especially to young people who don't have any idea of what is happening. People who continuously lie or manipulate the truth or use extreme sarcasm to get what they want are abusive. Habitual liars may or may not be aware of what they are doing. If called on their mistruths, most likely they will just brush it off like a "little white lie," something "everyone tells." Emotional abusers will do or say whatever it takes to achieve what they want. They may threaten to kill themselves if you leave them. Again, they are trying to manipulate you. Don't listen. Leave.

CHAPTER 49:
Communication

*"My wife says I never listen to her.
At least I think that's what she said."*

– Author unknown

Dear Lydia:

The ability to communicate with others is one of the most important things anyone will learn to develop in their lives. When most people think of communication, the first thing they think of their ability to speak. Obviously, that is crucial, but it's only a small part of communication. As I have watched you develop over your first fifteen months, I have seen you learn to communicate your various needs to me and others with very few words such as "hi," "mama," "dada," and "ball." Your learned mannerisms, such as excitedly pointing at food and say, "mmmm," communicated everything. On top of that, your beautiful smile says it all to me.

Many people would agree that the ability to communicate your needs is near the top of the list of essential things in any relationship. Remember, they are needs, not wants. Others would say that the inability to communicate is most often the most critical factor in relationships breaking up. This skill is so important that you should most definitely give it a lot of thought and maybe even practice it.

The best leaders communicate well. People may not agree with those leading them, but they should have a clear understanding of what the leader is saying and wants to be done. The key to leadership communication skills is the ability to listen. If a person does not feel like they're being heard, their need to communicate will shut down very quickly because their thinking becomes, "What difference does it make what I say? They're not listening anyway." I am always amazed when leaders think they are demonstrating great leadership skills but are indifferent to listening. As a basketball coach, one of my strengths was that I could give a pretty good motivational talk to my players to get them fired up to play a game, but it was just as important, if not more, that I needed to listen to their concerns and empathize with their parents.

While learning to communicate is an important skill to learn, many people also learn ways in which to derail communication or communication breakers. My guess is that some people who use these probably do not understand what they are doing to shut down communication. Perhaps they were not allowed to express their true feelings, and when they tried, they were chastised for it, so they internalized the belief that their opinion was not valued and that verbal communication in a civil manner was not allowed. What else did they learn? They learned that yelling is an effective way of communicating. They discovered that sarcasm works well too. When people suppress their feelings by saying things like, "I don't want to talk about it," or "I don't care," when they obviously do care, those suppressed emotions will reemerge at some point, perhaps years later. My advice to you is to learn how to communicate your feelings calmly without hurting someone else's feelings.

It has been said that guys have a more difficult time communicating than girls. I am not so sure about that, but I do understand it. Some say that girls are more in touch with their "emotional side" than guys are. Again, not always true. When you enter a long-term relationship, the ability for the two of you to communicate consistently without being locked into a score-keeping relationship, for example, "Well, I did this for you. Now you do that for me," goes a long way to establishing a healthy couple. At the same time, some people enjoy arguing with their partner. Some even say that it is good or "adds spice" to the relationship. They might even enjoy long, drawn-out debates with their partner. I disagree. My advice to you is to stay away from "win or lose" discussions. Win or lose is great on the basketball court, but it does not help your feelings for each other at all. In relationships, I think that if you need to win, you already lost.

As I said to you in an earlier chapter, one purpose of this book is to help you better understand yourself, who you are, and where you come from. One of the greatest strengths of your Great-Grandma Lydia Tank was her ability to communicate. As I grew up, I felt emotionally close to her, so I never felt uncomfortable sharing anything with her. We had good communication. I believe that your Grandma Becky and I passed that on to your mom and dad, and they will do the same for you. You are learning how to communicate effectively including expressing your feelings without judgment. Trust me, that is a true gift worth more than any amount of money.

CHAPTER 50:
Finding the Love of Your Life

"No road is long with good company."

– Turkish proverb

Dear Lydia:

If you have watched any movies targeted mainly to teenage girls, you will want to believe that there is that one extremely handsome guy out there who shares your every interest, who was put on earth just for you, and it is inevitable that your two paths will cross. He will fall totally in love with you and sweep you off your feet by never looking at another girl ever again. Money will never become an issue between the two of you because you are rich. You will get married in a lavish wedding while wearing an expensive white dress, have two kids, a boy and a girl, and he will take care of you forever. If that is your dream, you are not alone. Many girls grow up believing their "Prince Charming" fantasy. Of course, it is rare when it becomes a reality.

The first question you need to examine is whether or not there is such a thing as the "love of your life." Are you predestined to marry someone and have a family with them, or do things like that just happen randomly? Of course, I am not sure that there is a correct or incorrect answer to that question. It is one that has been asked for hundreds, if not thousands of years but has never been successfully answered. So, as with all the other chapters in this book, I will tell you what I think and give you my advice.

When I was in college at UW-Oshkosh, I became homesick like many first-year students. College life was difficult, and I went home on most weekends as did my roommate with whom I got along well. By the end of that first year, however, he decided that college was not for him, so he was going to drop out and return to his hometown and work in a factory. I started looking into transferring to Lakeland College, not far from home. I was even familiar with the campus because I had played a few basketball games there. I applied and got accepted and then was awarded a significant amount of scholarship money based on financial need as well as academic success. My parents were proud because there was a nice article about it in the local newspaper. As spring arrived and the school year wound down, I was all set and ready to move. But then, for some reason I will never understand, I decided to return to UW-Oshkosh for my sophomore year. It was a decision I never regretted. Two years later I met your Grandma Becky there, and we were married just after we graduated. I often wondered if some unknown force within me persuaded me to remain in Oshkosh. Had I left, my life would have changed radically.

An important consideration everyone must confront at some point is just how good-looking you are and how good-looking the person attracted to you will be. Somehow people of similar attraction find each other. In one experiment, ten men and ten women were put into a room each having a number from one through ten on their forehead. They could all see the numbers of everyone else but did not know their number. Their goal was to try to flirt or attract someone of the opposite sex with the highest number possible without anyone telling you what your number was. Hence, a number one or a two had no chance of attracting a nine or a ten. In the end, the results were, as expected, nearly all of the numbers were paired up exactly with their same number.

The big question for you in life becomes whether or not you will settle for anyone you do not consider to be a "ten." I have met some people who live long but lonely lives for that reason. My first piece of advice to you is be very wary of basing everything on a guy's looks. Second, to get the best possible guy, be the best possible girl. Third, have an idea in your head of the qualities your guy must have. One last point regarding looks. Studies have been done about guys who cheat on their wives. Studies have found that, contrary to what women may think, guys do not cheat on their wives because the other woman might be prettier or skinnier (most often the opposite is true). Guys cheat because of how the other woman makes him feel.

I hope you find the love of your life. To be deeply in love with the person who loves you is a true blessing. When I first dated your Grandma Becky, I asked her out the first time by sending her flowers on Valentine's Day. I didn't know her very well at the time, so when I signed the card "Chuck," she wasn't sure which Chuck it was! Eventually, we went out, and I knew very quickly that this was the woman I could be very serious about.

I believe that when you enter into a marriage, you are forming a deep commitment to that other person. You and your partner are forming a team that will confront life's issues together. Luckily in our family, divorce is not common. It has happened a few times but not a lot, for which I am glad. From what I understand, divorce is a very difficult thing to endure, and when children are involved, the consequences are magnified and can carry on into subsequent generations.

When my dad, Bill Tank, married my mom, Lydia Seidenzahl, shortly after the end of the Second World War in 1949, it was the beginning of a deep love relationship between the two of them. It would last until my mother's untimely death on September 4, 1980, at age fifty-nine. He was crushed by her death. I believe that had she lived for another twenty years or more, he would have too. (With advances in cardiac medicine over the next two decades, who knows how changes in lifestyle—they both smoked—could have lengthened their lives.) After hanging on in a coma for two weeks, she passed away, and when the life went out of her, it also went out of my dad. He lost his will to live when he lost the love of his life. I was newly married and in my second year of teaching. I was in no way prepared to watch my father give up his will to live. Within four months, he died on January 30, 1981, at age sixty-four. As I said in an earlier chapter, Tank men die young. As I look back on that episode in my life, and especially when I look at my ability to motivate people, I wish that I would have done more then to help motivate him.

Lydia, I hope I'm around to watch you walk down the aisle on your wedding day. Even if I'm not physically present, I will be with you in spirit. It's a big day. Talk to me if you want to, and I will do everything I can to answer you. Remember that it's about the long-term marriage, not just about the wedding day. Don't feel like you have to spend huge amounts of money just because it's "my day." I think the whole wedding industry is a racket, and you can give large amounts of money to people for some very unnecessary things. Your mom and dad were great with their wedding planning, and I trust that you will be too.

On a side note, certain things at weddings are symbolically important. For one thing, on my wedding day as my groomsmen and I were casually walking out of the back area of the church, and Grandma Becky's bridesmaids were walking down the aisle, I remember being nervous because this was it! I was about to get married. I recall it like it was yesterday. As I walked out of the back area of the church with the organ playing, I looked up, and the first person I saw sitting nearby was my mother, Lydia Tank (who I didn't realize had only nine months to live at that point). She looked me directly in the eyes and mouthed the words, "I love you" to me (just as I did to her nine months later as she lapsed into a coma). To me, it was like she knew she was handing the care of her son off to a woman in whom she had total trust. When you marry someone, it's not about impressing others with the amount of money you spent on your dress or the wedding reception or the size of the diamond in your wedding ring. It's about the commitment you feel to the guy you are going to be with for the next fifty years.

When I got married in 1979, my dad, Bill Tank, gave me my wedding ring. It was a ring handed down through the generations to me from his dad to him. He was born in 1916 in Sheboygan, so my guess is that it is well over one hundred years old. I wear it daily. To me, it is a symbol of my commitment to your Grandma Becky, whom I have been married to since 1979. It is a symbol to the endurance of our marriage into the twenty-first century.

CHAPTER 51:
Marriage

"A happy marriage is the union of two good forgivers."

– Ruth Bell Graham

Dear Lydia:

Everyone has their thoughts about marriage. Some views might be idealistic about spending the rest of your life with someone, while others are not so much. Most of those ideas are slowly formed and shaped in your mind over the years as you observed how your parents treated and interacted with each other. For a guy, how his dad treated his mother will have a significant impact on how he treats women. On the other hand, a girl keenly observes whether or not her mother is independent-minded or if she is more submissive to her husband's needs. All of the small day-to-day habits and rituals that everyone observes as they're growing up are brought into the marriage and form what will become their expectations and needs.

Of course, when I married your Grandma Becky at age twenty-three in December 1979 after dating for less than a year, I knew none of that. My older brother Mike and his wife, Cheryl, got married right out of high school when they were only nineteen, so I figured that I was "much older." Graduate from college, get a job, get married, and start a family. Don't mess with the order. As I saw it, that was the pattern, and, like most twenty-three-year-olds, I did not know what marriage was all about.

There are a number of different components that come together to form a marriage. One of the main components is the ability to compromise. If you need to be constantly right about everything, that puts your marriage at a big disadvantage. As I said earlier, the ability to communicate involves your ability to listen to your partner. If you cannot listen, you cannot communicate, and if you cannot communicate, you will likely be unable to compromise. In a marriage, that is a true disability. More than one marriage has ended because a wife or husband has said, "They were never wrong about anything. I was the one who always had to give in."

The second component of marriage is that you are sacrificing the "me" in the marriage for the "us" in the marriage. Some guys never understand that. Instead, they simply want to continue doing their "guy" things after they get married. This is where communication becomes crucial. If there is something that he does that bothers you, he may not know unless you tell him. He's not going to quit playing softball four nights a week plus weekend tournaments merely because he's now married. If you can find some common interests with him, you should focus on that. When your Grandma Becky and I got married, I would run four or five miles a day to stay in shape while also playing basketball and tennis. We found it really helped our relationship to set a common goal of running a marathon together, and we did it twice.

Your Great-Grandma Jeanne and Papa D dated throughout most of their high school years. After graduating, Great-Grandma Jeanne wanted to become a teacher because she liked little children. According to Papa D, "I wanted to go to college, but my dad needed my help milking cows and doing chores on the farm. I drove down to Normal every Friday or Saturday night to see her." The following year she was forced to put her schooling on hold because of money issues. Papa D started his own farm of eighty acres. "We didn't have any money to get married, so we didn't get married until 1951. We rented a house that had no running water, no indoor toilet, and no furnace. We had to carry our water in and out of the house. In 1954, when we bought the house we have now, we thought we were in Heaven."

Like people, all marriages evolve. This is not necessarily a bad thing. You mature, grow, and see things differently. So does your marriage. One thing which accelerates that evolution is when you start having children. Instead of your one-on-one relationship, now you are part of a triangle. Your children and your spouse have never-ending needs and expectations, which need to be met (if you have a job, then you have that to deal with). When you consider that triangle, do not forget about the bar in the triangle connecting you and your husband. Many times couples do that. They get so caught up in the other things in their lives that they forget to nurture that crucial part. At the same time, as you are running yourself ragged for everyone else, do not forget to take care of yourself and make sure your own needs are met.

When I tell you that you evolve in your marriage, I am not saying that you will love your husband less as time goes on. You will love him differently than you did during your early courtship, but you might even love him more. Within a short time, I will be married for thirty-eight years to your Grandma Becky. I do not doubt that she is the love of my life. I feel very fortunate that she agreed to go out with me those many years ago when we were students on the UW-Oshkosh campus.

When a couple gets married, no one thinks that they will get divorced. Of course, they hear all of the statistics about how half of all marriages end in divorce (that statistic has gone down in recent years). They get caught up in all of the wedding planning for "their day." Some go through pre-marital counseling to see if they are ready to marry that person. Divorce can be an ugly thing, and I don't wish it upon anyone, and I especially hope that you, Lydia, never experience the pain of divorce. I have a few things I would like to say to you about divorce. (By this point in the book, you are probably saying, "Of course you do, Grandpa Tank!")

First of all, unlike most people, I don't believe in the myth of the "surprise divorce." I do think that couples can become pretty good at disguising the problems which plague their marriages, but I have seen very few couples simply divorce "out of the blue." I think that if you care about your husband, and he cares about you, and you both put each other's needs before your own, that becomes apparent to others. If you don't do that, then the cracks within your marriage begin to form.

Sometimes marriage can be scary. I think there is often a feeling, perpetuated by the media (television used to do this more in the 1950s and 1960s) that everyone out there, especially your friends, has a great marriage, which will last blissfully for fifty years or more. I saw something once, however, that made much more sense to me. If you can picture a bar graph that is black on the right, gradually becoming gray in the middle, and is white on the left. The bar graph represents marriage. The black represents divorce, and the white represents the perfect marriage. The point is that there are very few perfect marriages. Most marriages are not so bad but not perfect. Most are somewhere in between the two. The point is, Lydia, a good marriage doesn't just happen naturally. It takes work!

As I said in an earlier chapter, Tank humor is incredibly funny (just ask me!). Some people believe that put-downs of others are a good form of humor. When I think back over the years to your Great-Grandpa Bill Tank, the funniest guy I have ever known, I cannot recall him ever using humor in which he put down his wife or any of us. Some very funny people do that, and I must admit that I have regretfully done that on occasion. My advice to you is not to do that. I have learned that if I am going to poke fun at someone, do it at myself, not anyone else. Put-downs of your spouse are not a good idea.

This is my last point regarding marriage. There are no easy answers, and I have just given you a few nuggets to ponder. You might meet the love of your life in high school like your Great Uncle Mike Tank did or like I did when I was in college. There are no guarantees. When you do meet him, however, please consider the advice I have given you in these pages. Unlike so many young people I have talked to recently, do not think you know everything as you get married. Remember that the people who act like they know a lot, usually don't. Learn from the people who have been there. They know.

CHAPTER 52:
A Final Letter to Lydia

"Goodbyes are not forever.
Goodbyes are not the end.
They simply mean I'll miss you,
until we meet again!"

– Author unknown

Dear Lydia:

By now you probably know that one of your great-grandmothers was also named Lydia. She was my mother and you are her namesake. She died when she was only fifty-nine years old, and I was too young to know much about anything, and remembering her, she probably knew that. However, she knew during her last years that she was living on borrowed time, and for some reason, she chose me as the person to relay certain things to the future generations. That is the primary reason for this book for which I give you credit for getting this far. Unlike all the earlier chapters in the book, this last chapter is written to her.

Dear Lydia Sophia Seidenzahl Tank, 1921–1980:

First of all, I have been dreading writing this last chapter and have been putting it off for weeks. How many people write a letter to their mother who has been dead for the last thirty-seven years? Another reason is that every time I think about what I would like to say to you, I get choked up and even a little teary-eyed. Yes, you meant that much to me, so this last chapter is meant for you.

There is a large tree next to my house that is much older than I am. It has aged well as it has grown upward reaching to the sky. I have watched the four seasons of each year come and go through the leaves of that tree. In the same area is my special "man cave" spot where I do the family grilling. (For years it was Johnsonville brats and Brennan's steak, but now it's more likely chicken breasts as I try to fight the dreaded genetically inherited heart disease.) Sometimes I have wondered if you have talked to me through that tree, and if so, what are you trying to tell me. When I coached basketball for so many years, I felt like you were telling me that it was a good thing. I was making a positive difference in the lives of high school kids. Now when I look up at the golden leaves swaying in the wind, I find myself thinking, "Mom, if I could talk to you now, what would you say to me?"

Throughout the last years of your life when I was much younger and living at home, I recall thinking that I should appreciate you because I did not know how much more time you had. It made me grow up in a hurry. After you died in 1980 when I was within my first year of marriage, I remember being sad but more so feeling a sense of, "Well, it finally happened." What took me so long to understand was how much I miss you. Today, it's rare that a day goes by without my thinking of you and something you once said or might have done. Another thing I often find myself asking is, "Why did you have to die so young?"

You were so wise, much wiser than I ever could appreciate. The values that you taught me through your words, actions, and life are still true today, and I find myself wondering if I became even half the parent to my three children that you were to me and my three brothers. I am so grateful for you teaching me the importance of communication. It seems like every other day I am talking to someone who has a problem with someone else, and the root of the issue is someone's inability to communicate.

Every time I see, hold, or even talk to Lydia Jeanne Alleman, your great-granddaughter, I cannot help but feel what a gift she is. Today, you would be ninety-seven years old, and I can only wish that you were here to give her a bite of German dessert and say to her, "Das schmechts gut!" as she loudly proclaimed, "mmmm." On the night of her birth after a very traumatic delivery, Dr. Barb Hostetler held and rocked the newborn Lydia Jeanne Alleman and whispered that she hoped that she was being named for a strong woman. Little did she know that she was being named for her two great-grandmothers, two women who were passing on wonderful traits of the Tank and Alleman families.

Acknowledgements

First and foremost, I want to thank my family for all of their help, thoughts, insights, and ideas. It's not always an easy thing to be interviewed by your dad and know that anything you say might go into print. My three children, Wes, Alli, and Ann all had interesting things to say to Lydia about the person she is and where she comes from.

A big thank you goes out to Scott and Diane Alleman as well as Scott's father, "Papa D" Alleman. They had many good things to say about Greg and the Alleman family, and it is apparent to me now why Greg Alleman, who was also a big help with this book, is the truly great person he is and a guy I am proud to call my son-in-law.

A special note of thanks goes out to Coach Joe Hanson who coached Lydia's mom, Ann, throughout her high school cross country and track career and Lauren Hawkinson, Ann's good friend growing up. Both were very insightful.

I am a reader. Books are a major part of my life. They make me think about who I am and the world in which I live. However, I have discovered that it's a lot easier reading books than writing them. Since writing *Coaching Our Sons* ten years ago, my wife, Becky, has been prodding me to write another. I resisted mostly because I wasn't sure what my topic should be. With the birth of my granddaughter, Lydia Jeanne Alleman, the light bulb came on. Throughout the process, no one encouraged me more than my wife, Becky. I thank her for that.

ALLEMAN-TANK FAMILY TREE

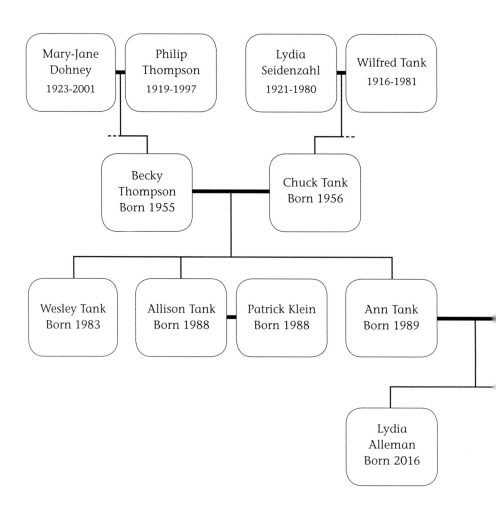

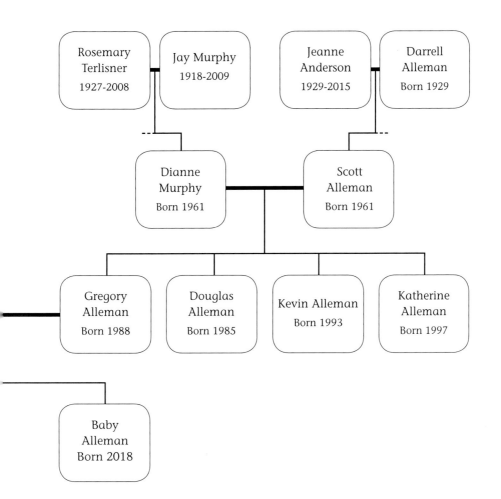

About the Author

Chuck Tank has taught history for thirty-nine years, most of that time at Dodgeville High School where he became a Hall of Fame basketball coach. He is the author of Coaching Our Sons, stories of basketball coaches who had their own children on their teams. Chuck and his wife of thirty-eight years, Becky, live in Dodgeville, Wisconsin, and are the parents of three, Wes, Alli Klein, and Ann Alleman. Lydia Alleman is their first grandchild.

Chuck, Becky, Patrick, Alli, Wes, Lydia, Ann, and Greg